COUNSELING
COLLEGE
STUDENTS

The Continuum Counseling Series

COUNSELING
COLLEGE
STUDENTS

*A Practical Guide for
Teachers, Parents,
and Counselors*

James Archer, Jr.
Foreword by William Van Ornum

Continuum | *New York*

1991

The Continuum Publishing Company
370 Lexington Avenue, New York, NY 10017

Copyright © 1991 by James Archer, Jr.
Foreword Copyright © 1991 by William Van Ornum

Printed in the United States of America

Library of Congress Cataloging-in-Publication Data

Archer, James.
    Counseling college students : a practical guide for teachers,
parents, and counselors / James Archer, Jr. ; foreword by William
Van Ornum.
       p. cm. — (The Continuum counseling series)
    ISBN 0-8264-0528-2
    1. Personnel service in higher education—United States.
    2. College students—United States—Counseling of. I. Title.
II. Series.
LB2343.A73 1991
378.1'94—dc20
                                            90-29007
                                                CIP

Contents

Foreword

The Continuum Counseling Series—the first of its kind for a wide audience—presents books for everyone interested in counseling, bringing to readers practical counseling handbooks that include real-life approaches from current research. The topics deal with issues that are of concern to each of us, our families, friends, acquaintances, or colleagues at work.

General readers, parents, teachers, social workers, psychologists, school counselors, nurses and doctors, pastors, and others in helping fields too numerous to mention will welcome these guidebooks that combine the best professional learnings and common sense, written by practicing counselors with expertise in their specialty.

Increased understanding of ourselves and others is a primary goal of these books—and greater empathy is the quality that all professionals agree is essential to effective counseling. Each book offers practical suggestions on how to "talk with" others about the theme of the book, be this in an informal and spontaneous conversation or a more formal counseling session.

Professional therapists will value these books also, because each volume in The Continuum Counseling Series develops its subject in a unified way, unlike many other books that may be either too technical or, as edited collections of papers, may come across to readers as being disjointed. In recent years both the American Psychological Association and the American Psychiatric Association have endorsed books that build on the scientific traditions of each profession but are communicated in an interesting way to general readers. We hope that professors and students in fields such as psychology, social work, psychiatry, guidance and counseling, and other helping fields will find these books to be helpful companion readings for undergraduate and graduate courses.

From nonprofessional counselors to professional therapists,

from students of psychology to interested lay readers, The Continuum Counseling Series endeavors to provide informative, interesting, and useful tools for everyone who cares about learning and dealing more effectively with these universal, human concerns.

Counseling College Students

In *Counseling College Students* Jim Archer's dedication, insights, and great respect for college students are bountiful. This is a book that will help everyone on the campus—professors, administrators, dorm personnel, chaplains, resident assistants—as well as parents and other counselors to whom college students may be referred. Dr. Archer believes that much of the counseling on campus takes place with concerned adults who are part of the campus experience; however, detailed information is given on how to refer students for more specialized help when this is needed.

Before we can counsel college students, it is important to understand the life issues they face, and the book presents an overview of developmental tasks, and looks at areas such as adult students who are returning after working or raising a family, students from minority groups, and other unique situations as well. Information about counseling is given, and Dr. Archer encourages the many adults who are present on the college campus but who may not be professional counselors by noting "psychologists, psychiatrists, and other mental health counselors spend years learning how to provide effective counseling and psychotherapy, yet much of the basic process of counseling is not all that complicated. As a faculty member, relative, friend, or advisor you can learn to be very helpful to college students by being a wise and understanding listener."

The book brings us into the world of the student. For many who may have forgotten, the importance of academic success is described; going beyond empathy, the excellent chapter on "Academic Success" provides practical strategies in areas such as time management, study skills, and reading that will help the helpers empower the students with whom they work. Career choice is an area that often puts the student in a quandary. They spin their wheels, trying to decide on whether to be a doctor or lawyer or writer. Dr. Archer suggests ways that "counselors and students can pick two or three possible choices and develop a set of activities and courses which will help keep the students' options open for a while."

For many students, being in college is one of the most important times in life for learning about relationships, from friendship to love, and the book gives an in-depth treatment on helping students grapple with the relationship issues they face. Ways that help students "change their thinking" and make positive changes in their behavior are presented. A chapter on "sexuality" is another helpful feature.

In the latter part of the book, we learn of approaches to stress management and how to handle some of the more difficult situations that may be encountered on a college campus, such as depression and suicide, eating disorders, and alcohol and substance abuse. Again, the importance of appropriate referral is discussed.

As a psychologist who teaches at a college, I found *Counseling College Students* helpful, wise, and thought-provoking. Everyone from experienced counselors to persons just beginning their work in the exciting atmosphere of a college environment (such as resident advisors) will want to read this book. In clear language Dr. James Archer brings us into the world of college students, and suggests ways for us to help them lead a balanced and fulfilling life in college—no small achievement, as these same skills will help them throughout life after college.

William Van Ornum, Ph.D.
Marist College
Poughkeepsie, New York

General Editor
The Continuum Counseling Series

Preface

This book is written for anyone who counsels college students or who wants to understand them better. Counseling is defined broadly here as any listening, advice-giving, or helping activity. In addition to professional counselors and psychologists, non-professional helpers like advisors, parents, faculty members, friends, and many others can be very effective in a helping, counseling role. In fact, most students don't go to psychologists or professional counselors for personal and emotional help. They usually turn to friends and other nonprofessionals.

If you are in one of these nonprofessional helping roles, this book should increase your knowledge about college student psychological development and also help you become a better listener, helper, and counselor. Whether you are a friend, faculty member, or advisor, there is a great deal that you can do to be helpful to college students. I don't, however, mean to encourage you to try to handle problems that should be handled by a professional. In fact, one entire chapter in this book is devoted to sources of professional help and how to make referrals.

This book may also be helpful to professional counselors and therapists who work with college students; however, it is not a technical book with new theories about therapy with college students. It is rather a recording of my observations and experiences over about twenty years as a college counselor. It is written in a conversational manner, and I hope that this informality will help with the communication process between reader and author.

Let me say something about myself. I am forty-seven years old, white, male, married happily for nineteen years, with two children. I used to feel like a fellow student when I counseled young college students. Somewhere along the way I began feeling more like a parent. I don't claim to have any profound hold on psychological health. I have my ups and downs, my times of stress, depression, hopelessness, and exhilaration, just like everybody else. I do feel that I know a lot about what it takes to be psychologically healthy; and over the years I've come to believe that I'm pretty good at helping students move in that direction. Sometimes, I can even use what I know to help myself.

I suppose it takes a fair amount of egocentrism to write a book like this. After all, do I really know enough to offer myself as an expert and an author? Evidently the answer is yes, or you wouldn't be reading this. Much of what I do know comes from my interactions with others. One of the things that attracted me to psychology and to counseling is a fascination with how people operate. I love to watch people and to talk with them. On an individual level they usually seem basically good to me, yet the evil and pathology in our society often bother and disturb me.

Well, enough about me. Let me say one more thing about this book. It's mostly made possible by the hundreds, probably thousands, of clients with whom I have talked over the years. I am constantly amazed at their trust, their vulnerability, and their strength. Sometimes the secrets they tell me are awe inspiring. I am overwhelmed by their trust in me and often enraged, perplexed, and saddened by what they have had to go through. My friends and my colleagues have also greatly influenced me. They have often taught me what to do and what not to do. Finally, my wife and my children are a special part of me that is strongly connected to my work and to my understanding of human relationships.

1

College Students

College students come in all shapes, sizes, and colors. They may be eighteen or they may be thirty-eight. Statisticians tell us that, in the 1990s, more and more minorities and nontraditional-age students will be going to college. Today, disabled students are attending college and taking advantage of equipment and facilities that didn't exist just a few years ago. There is much greater diversity than ever before, yet we still consider college students as a group. Are they really different from other people of the same age and circumstances? The answer is both yes and no. People attending college have many things in common with those who do not attend. In that sense, much of what is discussed in this book applies to everyone. On the other hand, college students are distinct from other groups because they are undertaking a fairly specific set of learning experiences. Their expectations about life and about themselves are colored by what they expect of a "college education" and by what is expected of them.

Before beginning a discussion of college students and their environment, let me take some time to introduce my plan for this book. Chapter 2 includes a description of the counseling process and in chapter 11 I discuss the referral process. The emphasis in these two chapters is on helping you understand the basic process of counseling, how to refer, and how to identify your own limits as a counselor. Chapters 1 and 3 focus on students themselves: their makeup, personality, and general environment. Chapters 4, 5, 6, and 7 deal with major developmental issues that are almost always very significant for college students: basic study skills, career and life goals, relationships, and sexuality. Often problems in these areas can be of great concern to students, and an inability to handle them can lead to failure and serious psychological problems. In the remaining chapters, some of the most common and most difficult problems facing college students are discussed. These include identity, self-concept, and interpersonal problems resulting from growing up in alcoholic and dysfunctional families; substance abuse; stress; depression; suicide; and eating disorders.

In this first chapter, I hope to provide a general description of college students and their world. Given the great diversity of students and colleges, that is no easy task. Two approaches seem to make sense. One is to provide an overview of the major developmental issues that college students experience, and the other is to describe some of the changes and challenges that are created by the college environment.

Developmental Issues

Developmental issues are the tasks or common experiences encountered by people of roughly similar ages. For example, young people face similar tasks and experiences when they pass through adolescence. They have to learn to cope with new feelings about sexuality, they must begin to develop a sense of identity, and they are expected to become young adults. Similarly, people around the age of sixty-five must learn to cope with the physical aspects of old age, and also with the idea of retirement and rather different life-styles. These developmental issues are usually a result of both biological change and social expectations. For the adolescent, there is significant biological change, and also important new social and role expectations. For the retiring person, the process of physically growing old is an important factor, as are changing social and role expectations.

Many of the problems that college students experience relate to developmental tasks. If you understand what it is like for people who are at a particular level of development, you will be a step closer to understanding their world as they see it. Since most college students are in their late teens or early twenties, it is particularly important to understand what goes on for people during those years. However, to counsel and understand older adult college students, you must also have some understanding of adult development throughout the life span. Since Freud first presented his ideas on how very early childhood development affected a person's psychological development, there has been a gradual trend toward the realization that we all undergo significant psychological development throughout life. It is only in the past fifteen years or so that psychologists have begun to focus seriously on development in the later adult years.

My strategy here will be to discuss a number of developmental issues; and describe how those issues relate to development during the traditional college years and also how they get played out over the entire life span. Before doing that, however, let me introduce an example that shows how difficult developmental issues can be for a student, and how difficult it can be if he or she isn't able to meet the generally accepted timetable for development. There are actually great variations in how people develop, but our tolerance for variation is often not great:

> Henry is a senior in college. He will graduate in May with a degree in business. He sought out counseling because he was feeling a great deal of anxiety and was unable to sleep at night. His grades were suffering and he wasn't doing much in the way of searching for future employment. Henry was feeling the pressure of graduating. His parents have often urged him to date more often and had expected him to be engaged, or at least have a permanent relationship, by now. Henry hasn't really dated in college. He majored in business without giving it too much thought and now he isn't really sure what he wants to do. He is a tall, good-looking young man, about 6'1", and everyone (mostly his relatives) tells him that he has a great future and that he would be a wonderful "catch" for some lucky woman.

In this example, it isn't too difficult to see how age-related social expectations are putting rather strong pressures on Henry. He isn't quite ready to take up the expected role yet. Even his physical growth works against him, because he is deemed physically ready and able to proceed. Henry needs to discuss his own developmental progress and perhaps figure out why he isn't ready to seek employment or develop relationships. He may not yet have solidified an identity for himself, he may not have the skills to interact with women, or he may not really want to go into business as a career.

Now that you see how difficult the timing of developmental tasks can be, let me go on and discuss several different developmental themes. These will include identity, relationships/intimacy, career/life goals, and morality/philosophy of life. Also, I want to spend some time looking at special developmental issues related to minority status and sex roles. Although I will be examining these issues in age-related terms, please remember that, in addition to understanding how general developmental tasks and pressures affect students, you must also have a deep appreciation for the differences between students in terms of timing and even the extent of developmental experiences. An eighteen-year-old may have a stronger sense of identity and be able to relate to others in more effective ways than a twenty-five-year-old graduate student. You can't assume that everyone is moving along at the same pace, yet you need to pay attention to the general age ranges and social forces.

Identity

Men and women have been searching for their "identity" for centuries. Part of being human seems to involve being able to develop a sense of self or identity. Although the idea has been around for centuries, Erik Erikson, a twentieth-century psychologist, popularized the term and described the interaction between social and biological forces that forms identity. He saw identity formation as the major developmental task of adolescence, with the young person involved in a struggle between identity (defined roles) and role diffusion (very different possibilities).

More recent psychological theory has explained the different ways that males and females go through this developmental stage and also the way in which identity issues are played out in later adulthood. The now well-known midlife crisis, for example, is a kind of revisitation of identity questions for people in their early forties. Identity questions and issues often recur several times in a person's lifetime and questions like, "Who am I?" or "What do I really want?" are not uncommon. Nonetheless, a kind of basic identity, or perhaps "foundation identity," is generally formed during one's teens or early twenties.

One way of viewing identity is to divide up a person's life into the different roles that he or she typically plays in our society. A person, then, must have an identity in each of several areas: career, sexual, moral, interpersonal, political, intellectual, and even recreational. Traditional-age college students (eighteen–twenty-two) are often still involved in exploring and solidifying their identity in these areas. Much of the anxiety, stress, and depression that these students experience is related to progress or lack of progress. For example, a junior in college who still hasn't selected a major is likely to experience considerable anxiety and feel pressure to set goals and make career choices. Or, a student who has been brought up in a strict fundamentalist religion, and encounters roommates who challenge his or her beliefs on every front, will certainly feel the stress and pressure from conflicting belief systems.

Part of the whole process of identity formation is a gradual breaking away from parents, however, sometimes this process can be abrupt. Ideally, this move toward independence happens throughout a student's teen years and by the time he or she enters college the student has developed considerable self-sufficiency. Even in the best of cases, however, this process is not a smooth one. A certain amount of anger and conflict with parents seems to be inevitable and probably necessary.

College students sometimes need a great deal of help during this final transitional period to adulthood. Contact with an adult, other than parents, can be enormously helpful to students who are sorting out major identity issues. Often, all that is needed is an understanding and compassionate listener who is heavy on understanding and light on advice giving.

But what about nontraditional-age students? They are not at the end of their teens, finishing up what society has proscribed as a normal developmental process. They come from all walks of life. They may be in their late twenties, having decided late to come to college; they may be in their late thirties or forties, coming back to school after raising a family; or they may have experienced a midforties identity crisis and decided to make a major career switch. Clearly, their identity questions are different. Although these returning adults come from many different walks of life, they all have some identity concerns in common as a result of going back to college. Almost by definition, the decision to go to a college or university affects one's identity. This activity is such a major life endeavor that it almost always carries with it expectations for change, improvement, and new challenges and rewards. It also almost always involves some difficult changes. College for returning adults is often an activity that must be managed within the context of many other family responsibilities. Returning adult students need teachers, advisors, and other staff to help them explore their new direction and all of the new behaviors and requirements that they are facing.

Much of what I have described above is what normally happens to college students in their search for life goals, career, and identity. Under the best of circumstances, when a person has a strong sense of self-worth and a sound and loving family background, the development of identity and choices surrounding it can be difficult and painful. When a person has family or other psychological problems interfering, the growth and development of identity can be considerably more difficult. A young woman who has been sexually molested as a child will inevitably have to deal with this experience before she can formulate a healthy identity and sense of self. A man who grew up in a home with an alcoholic parent will have to deal with and confront how those experiences affected him, and how they are interfering with his growth and functioning as a human being. With the alcohol, drug, and family problems existing in our present culture, it is not unusual for a student, either traditional age or adult, to have to deal with negative past experiences that interfere with growth and identity development. Additionally, some college students have personality disorders and other serious psychological problems that make progress for them impossible. As a potential counselor of college students, you must understand the complexities of dealing with identity and particularly with problems blocking identity formation. Remember that, for most students, basic listening and counseling can be enormously helpful; but for some, professional help is needed.

Before leaving the topic of identity, I want to discuss briefly the male-female differences in identity formation and how being a minority student can affect identity. As a counselor, you need to understand something about sex role socialization. The development and formation of identity for both men and women can be unnecessarily restricted by sex role stereotypes and restrictions. For example, a young woman who has never been encouraged to set difficult goals may find it hard to think about medicine as a career. Or a man who is naturally warm, sensitive, and emotional may have trouble incorporating these characteristics into his identity. A counselor cannot provide resocialization for students who are caught in the restrictions of sex role limitations, but he or she can challenge and discuss these restrictions during conversations with students.

Young women in particular are often coping with conflicts and decisions about the changing roles for women and how to fit into the expanding but demanding new possibilities. Some developmental theorists say that female identity development is different from males. Female identity seems to be more related to relationships and sharing of self, while male identity is more related to the traditional notion of becoming independent and self-sufficient. A counselor must be wary of preconceived notions of what should happen because of a person's sex. There are basic differences *between* men and women as well as great differences *among* men and women.

Minority students must struggle with powerful identity issues related to their ethnic or racial identity and their identity as part of a majority culture. Most minority students entering college have aspirations not unlike those of the majority of students. They want a happy and fulfilled life with a good job and a secure future. But they are also quite different from majority students. Their backgrounds are often different and they may not have the same values or social customs. At predominantly white institutions, they must learn how to compete in the majority culture while still maintaining a separate cultural identity. Theories of racial identity have been developed to help explain how the interaction between white and black cultures affects the identity development of African-American students. These students must also deal with racism and general expectations that they may not be as academically able as their majority counterparts. Other minorities, like disabled students or gay/lesbian students, also have unique identity issues to handle. In general, white/majority culture counselors and advisors can be helpful to minority students, but these students also need to have close contact with adults and successful role models like themselves.

Career, Interpersonal, and Moral Development

Although career, interpersonal, and moral development, are all crucial parts of identity development, I have chosen to discuss them briefly as separate developmental themes. Many of the problems and issues that students experience in these areas will be discussed in greater detail in later chapters. **Career development** is clearly a major issue for traditional-age and adult college students. In most cases, students come to college with a career goal in mind or they expect to be able to find a viable career as a result of college attendance. Although there are many purely educational advantages to going to college, most people in our society still see college attendance as related in some way to career achievement. Many times, students suffer from too strong a career emphasis. These students take a narrow view of their college experience and miss many educational and personal growth opportunities. Other students experience a great deal of stress and pressure to perform, usually as a result of growing up in families where career and academic achievement are highly prized.

Parents, faculty, and society at large often have great difficulty coming to grips with the fact that career choice occurs on many different timetables. Not all students are ready to choose a career during the first two years of college. Nonetheless, students must cope with a very intense pressure to choose a goal and career. Of course, having a goal in mind can be enormously helpful in terms of academic success and personal development, so there are certainly rewards for being able to choose. Other aspects of identity, however, must be reasonably well jelled. If major blocks to identity development in any area exist, it may be difficult for a student to approach career decisions.

Relationships are important to all of us. Human beings all have a need for close, intimate relationships, and most of us search for intimate relationships that also have a healthy sexual component. Traditional-age college students in their late teens and early twenties are just beginning to learn how to form healthy and reciprocal intimate relationships. The independence that many experience as they enter college often has a profound effect on their relationships. They usually no longer have parents to provide a close advising or monitoring function.

This results in considerable experimentation and sometimes rather extreme sexual and interpersonal behavior. For other students who have not learned relationship skills or who are so confused about their own identity that they can't really deal with intimate or close relationships, the college experience becomes a lonely and interpersonally unsuccessful time. They see people all around them enjoying each other, but they can't manage it for themselves.

For older, adult students, the interpersonal issues are quite different. In fact, it is difficult to generalize because adult students come from so many different walks of life. Attending college does require an adult student to make and form new relationships. For many, the first weeks and months are full of anxiety since they are returning to school to compete with youngsters they see as sharper and more accustomed to studying and learning. Returning adults may feel somewhat out of place in a classroom filled with nineteen-year-olds. A returning adult student's present relationships are usually affected by his or her decision to attend college. Certainly his or her spouse, lovers, and children must learn new ways to relate in order to cope with major relationship changes. For example, the wife who returns to school after raising her family may develop new ideas and a new sense of identity that can profoundly change a long-standing marriage relationship.

For traditional-age students, college is often a time for experimentation and for selecting a personal set of values. Although most students end up with a sense of **morality and values** similar to their parents, in the college years they must integrate what they have learned while growing up into their own value system and sense of self. Courses, instructors, and other students frequently challenge a student's current sense of morality. I still remember vividly my freshman English instructor who delighted in challenging long-held religious beliefs as we studied the Bible as literature. I also remember my first encounter with someone who was cheating, and listening to a rather elaborate rationalization for his behavior. These challenges, along with an increasing ability to see the complexities of different issues, tend to move college students toward a less dualistic and more pluralistic way of viewing morality. On the other hand, some students who feel very disoriented because of their loss of a kind of right and wrong grounding can be drawn to religious groups and sects that offer an absolute set of rules and standards. The sense of morality and values that a student develops becomes an important part of his or her identity. Our view of the world and our reaction to it are strongly influenced by what we value and consider moral and right.

College Environment

To understand the college environment you have to be able to imagine what it is like for a new student who encounters the many changes and challenges involved. As a counselor, you may be tempted to compare your own experience with that of current students. This can be helpful, but you must also remember that each person's experience is very different, even if he or she is reacting to similar circumstances. You may have found sorority life a wonderful and enriching experience, but someone else may find it limiting and unpleasant.

Change is one environmental experience with which all students must contend. Things are always changing. For many, this change is something that they have looked forward to with eager anticipation; for others, it is something that they have dreaded and worried about. The "change" factor most affects new students. They tend to encounter all of the changes and new situations simultaneously, and this often creates a period of disorganization and stress. Environmental changes, of course, take place all during the college years—new courses, new professors, new friends, etc., but the magnitude of change at the beginning is very different.

The challenge of academic work is an ongoing experience felt by almost all students. Along with this challenge is often an intense sense of anxiety and fear about whether or not one is up to the challenge. Competition does increase and students who have been at the top of their high school classes are now competing with others of comparable ability. In addition to this overall feeling about a different and more difficult set of academic challenges come all of the actual challenges—lecture classes, sometimes indifferent and demanding professors, final exams, long papers, difficult labs, and so on. To understand the academic pressures on a particular student you have to imagine how this aspect interacts with all the other challenges in the environment. This requires you to understand the individual student's frame of reference. A seventeen-year-old freshman worrying about making friends, how he looks, meeting women, studying engineering, and missing his parents has one frame of reference; while a forty-two-year-old master sergeant recently coming back to school, worrying about how her family will like the new community, how she will compete with seventeen-year-olds, and how her daughter will do in the new high school has another.

Socially, the college environment can be quite different. Often there is a need to meet new people, form new relationships, and develop a new support system. Students sometimes report that they feel lonely and isolated even though they are in a sea of people most of the time. For many, it is difficult to operate in this new social environment. If one is not in some kind of group with ready access to other students, it can be difficult to meet people and form new relationships. Returning adults must cope with juggling their already formed relationships with new ones. They don't have as much time for family and friends; they can't do all the things that they have done before.

For most students, going to college involves a new living situation. Whether it is a traditional dormitory or an apartment with several roommates, the challenge of forging effective roommate relationships and developing a living style that is productive and balanced is very important. The influence of roommates can be strong and the disruption caused by having a roommate who isn't compatible can be very disheartening. As with many aspects of college, the relationship that one can have with a roommate is often idealized. Students imagine that their college roommate will become one of their closest friends and that the friendship will last a lifetime. This may happen, but it is certainly not a sure thing. Just having a roommate or roommates can be difficult for many students who are used to having a room of their own and considerable privacy. The lack of private space can be very disconcerting to someone who is used to recharging his or her batteries by having time alone.

Although I have tried to generalize about college students and their environment, each student has a unique set of developmental issues and encounters the college environment in a particular way. A general understanding of the major environmental challenges can help you, as a counselor, understand students, but there is no substitute for really trying to understand what the college experience is like for each individual student.

2

Basic Counseling

Psychologists, psychiatrists, and other mental health counselors spend years learning how to provide effective counseling and psychotherapy, yet much of the *basic* process of counseling is not all that complicated. As a faculty member, relative, friend, or advisor you can learn to be very helpful to college students by being a wise and understanding listener. Although the process of basic counseling and listening is not complicated, it is also not easy. You need to develop the skills and insight to do it well. The purpose of this chapter is to outline some of the basic skills and behaviors that make a good "counselor." I do this with some reservation because I know that many students need more than just "basic" counseling, and I know that there are many complex and useful theories of counseling and psychotherapy that go well beyond what I plan to discuss. Also, I should note that I am referring here to individual, one-on-one counseling, not group counseling.

Since my purpose is to help many different kinds of people learn to be better counselors to college students, I will outline some of the basic principles of good counseling and at the same time discuss limits and situations when more than just a basic approach is needed. For most college students, effective listening and support in sorting through alternatives and possible changes can be enormously helpful. Human beings, including college students, have great potential to improve and chart their own growth. For some reason, our colleges and universities don't provide many opportunities for students to talk with faculty or other adults about their personal feelings and problems. I am continually struck by the fact that so many students come into my counseling office and disclose thoughts, feelings, and problems that they just haven't been able to discuss with anyone else. I am thankful that I am there to help them, but I am also a bit sad that of all the people in their lives there was no one with whom they could really talk. Since I am a trained psychologist I can usually key into their issues quickly and help them begin to move in a positive direction, but many of them could also be helped by an interested and willing faculty member, friend, minister, or other college staff member. Although our society has developed a large cadre of professional counselors and therapists, there are still not enough of us to counsel and listen to everyone who needs it.

At the risk of greatly oversimplifying, I have outlined seven steps for effective counseling. These steps are basic, and have been described in various ways in many studies and books. These steps include the following:

1. Listen and establish a working relationship.
2. Develop a focus.
3. Contract to counsel the student or refer him or her to a professional.
4. Establish realistic alternatives and goals.
5. Devise an action plan.
6. End counseling and evaluate.

(1) Listen and Establish a Working Relationship

Define the relationship. Before you can do any counseling, you have to provide the right setting and establish some agreement on what is going to occur. Counseling is defined as one person helping another person. Therefore, you must agree upon roles. Counseling is not a free-flowing conversation where each person tells about his or her problems. Not that this can't be helpful or enjoyable—it just isn't counseling. Counseling may evolve from a conversation, but there needs to be a clear signal that the interaction has moved from a conversation to counseling. For example, if a student is talking with a faculty member after class and begins to discuss a personal problem he or she has with another student, the faculty member should, at some point, decide whether or not he or she wants to counsel the student. If the faculty member does, then an appropriate statement might be, "It sounds like you would like to talk about your problems with anxiety. I have some time now. Would you like to talk?" An alternate response might be, "Look, I can tell that you need to talk with someone about your feelings. Can we set up a time tomorrow and I will be glad to discuss the situation with you?" Although it happens very frequently, I don't think that it is a good idea to slide into a counseling or helping role without some understanding and agreement by both parties. You don't have to be overly formal about it, but some acknowledgment is really useful. Even when two friends are talking and one is in need of counseling or just a sympathetic ear, one person needs to take the role of helper and one of helpee. Sometimes one friend will wind up not wanting to be "counselor" to another friend all of the time. This usually happens when there is no discussion or acknowledgment about the role of helper (counselor) and helpee (person with a problem to discuss). One other important point: by agreeing to listen to what is troubling someone you are not necessarily agreeing to spend the next three months being his or her counselor. In fact, you may very soon decide that you cannot deal with the problem and suggest a referral. You do, however, need to realize that once a person opens up to you, you have some obligation to help see him or her through, at least until he or she can find help elsewhere. If you don't really want to get involved, don't.

I said earlier that any friend, faculty member, college staff member, or family member can be helpful and serve in some capacity as a student's counselor. Let me include some reservations now that have to do with roles. In many close relationships it is difficult or impossible to serve as a counselor or helper to another person. Parents, for example, often cannot serve as counselors to their own children, or husbands to wives, or friends to each other. The emotional connections and closeness often make it difficult for the listener or counselor to perform effectively in that role. Keep in mind that emotional complications can make some helping relationships impossible. Also, remember that one of the great benefits of a professional counselor or therapist is that he or she is already in a kind of helping and objective role. Faculty members, student personnel workers, ministers, and student counselors provide a certain level of objectivity.

Once the parameters of a counseling relationship have been established, you need to worry about some mundane issues like where you are going to talk. Counseling sessions need to be held in a private place where there will be no interruptions. Again, some definition of what is going to occur will help you set the stage and find an appropriate setting. Privacy and attention help a person focus on his or her problems and they help you as the counselor attend to the person 100 percent. A private office or room isn't the only possible setting, and there are times when other settings must be used, but the more private and comfortable the better. The issue of time is also important. If you are going to talk with a student about a particular issue you need to think about how much time you have to give. Don't get started listening to a student who has an emotional issue to discuss if you only have ten minutes to spare. Although it may be difficult not to be immediately responsive, you will be better off and more effective if you ask the student to come back when you can give him or her enough time.

Good listening is probably the most, or at least one of the most, crucial parts of counseling. In order to be a good listener you must be completely attuned to what the other person is saying. You must realize that your own needs to talk, share stories, and give advice will have to take second place, at least for the time being, in order to really hear the other person.

Attend to your nonverbal behavior. Your nonverbal behavior is very important. Some very good listeners don't say much at all. They express their caring and concern partly by the way they communicate without words. To do this you must face the person, have good eye contact, and express your interest and openness by your body. Head nods and other small gestures often communicate that you are listening and following. If you haven't had any formal training in counseling it may be difficult for you to assess just how well you communicate nonverbally. Consider two levels of this behavior. The first level involves your basic body orientation to the other person and is partly related to how you set up a counseling session. If you try to counsel students from behind a desk or in a setting that doesn't have comfortable chairs with a comfortable space between them, you are not providing a good, open counseling situation. Having a desk between you and someone you hope to counsel tends to decrease the effectiveness of nonverbal communication. If you are a professor, administrator, or someone who talks with students in your office where you also have a desk, you should arrange chairs somewhere else for counseling purposes.

An assessment of more subtle nonverbal behavior really requires some kind of formal feedback so that you can actually see yourself and learn how your nonverbal behavior affects others. Videotaping yourself while conversing with someone will give you some idea of how you communicate nonverbally. Also, asking friends or colleagues about how you look when you are listening to them will give you some clues. Because faculty and staff in colleges and universities are often quite verbally oriented they sometimes ignore the importance of the nonverbal aspects of communication behavior. You can help yourself considerably in your role as counselor and helper if you take time to examine and evaluate your nonverbal behavior.

Practice active listening. Nonverbal behavior, however, isn't enough by itself. The student must perceive that you understand what he or she is saying and feeling. Asking for help or telling someone about a personal problem can be quite scary, and the counselee often watches the counselor closely for signs that the counselor is really understanding him or her. Verbal responses that indicate the counselor's understanding are very important. The process of giving these verbal responses is called *active listening*. This means that you, as a listener, periodically let the other person know that you are following and understanding him or her. This is done most effectively by what is called a "reflection." A reflection is basically paraphrasing what a person has just said. For counseling purposes, paraphrases usually focus on what feelings the other person has expressed. By letting the student know that you have some understanding of his or her feelings you are able to demonstrate your "empathic understanding" of him or her. Since every person and every student thinks and feels in some unique ways, it is essential for a counselor to try to understand this uniqueness and the student's special frame of reference. Following are two examples of paraphrasing and reflection of empathic understanding. (Note how the empathic responses encourage the student to explore the situation and his or her feelings further.)

Example 1

STUDENT: I just can't follow what the professor is saying. He goes so fast and never stops to see if anyone has any questions. Sometimes I think I will stand up in class and scream.

COUNSELOR: You are *really* frustrated with this situation and sometimes feel like you can't take it any more.

Example 2

STUDENT: I don't know what is wrong. I just don't feel very happy anymore. I even start to cry for no reason.

COUNSELOR: You seem to be very sad and maybe depressed, and you can't seem to figure out why.

As you read these examples, remember that paraphrasing is something that you particularly need to do during step 1 of a counseling situation. It helps you establish rapport and build a working relationship. You wouldn't necessarily continue with this paraphrasing forever. Also, using paraphrasing sounds and feels awkward to many people. You will have to adapt it to your own style. Don't reject it, though, without trying it out and experimenting with how you can implement it. The process of paraphrasing, by requiring you to come up with a succinct restatement of the student's feelings, will challenge you to listen more closely. In other words, this method forces you to try harder to be empathic.

Don't give advice too soon. During the initial phase of counseling, there are a number of responses that tend to interfere with the development of a good working relationship. One very common mistake is to give advice too soon. Although a student may actually come to you for advice, unless you listen and really hear what is bothering him or her your advice will have limited value. Often students receive advice from too many others, when what they really want is to feel understood and to have someone help them figure out solutions for themselves. We all like to come up with our own solutions and often a solution or course of action is only meaningful and useful after we have worked it out in our own minds. Premature advice giving in a counseling situation forecloses this possibility and it also prevents a listener from establishing an effective working relationship.

Don't be judgmental. Being judgmental can also abruptly stop the development of rapport that is the hallmark of a good counseling/helping relationship. If a student tells you about something that you believe is wrong, stupid, or dangerous, a judgmental response can stop communication. Following are two examples of *inappropriate* judgmental statements.

Example 1

> STUDENT: After I took her home I went out and got really drunk, then I drove home and slept it off. Boy, did I have a hangover that next morning.
>
> COUNSELOR: Terry, I thought you were smarter than that. Don't you know that it is very dangerous to drink and drive?

Example 2

> STUDENT: I am really scared about being pregnant. How can I have a baby when I'm not even finished with college? I don't know what to do or how I feel.
>
> COUNSELOR: You do sound confused, but I am sure that you don't want to consider abortion. Let's talk about some other options.

In example 1, the counselor is certainly right; drinking and driving are very dangerous, but what needs to be explored at this point is Terry's feelings and his motivation for drinking. If Terry has an alcohol problem you, as the counselor, are much more likely to get him to confront his dangerous behavior *after* you have established a working relationship and have established yourself as someone who cares and understands some of the reasons for his drinking. In example 2, the counselor is more subtle about expressing her judgment. In this case, she steers the client away from considering all options and from freely expressing her feelings about these options. Although counseling is never really value-free, the counselor has an obligation not to impose his or her values on a student who is coming for help. Later on in the helping relationship the counselor can point out the consequences of different choices and behavior, and perhaps even give his or her opinion, but only after the relationship has been established.

Don't talk about yourself. Focus on the person you are counseling. One other trap into which many novice counselors blunder is bringing in a similar situation or feeling from their own life. In general, this is not appropriate in the early stages of counseling. The focus must remain on the student who is being counseled. Bringing in your own experiences can be appropriate sometimes later on in counseling. However, in this early stage it will only distract you and the student from dealing with the problem at hand.

Don't ask too many questions. Generally it is better to paraphrase or nod your head to encourage a person to continue talking. Direct questions can distract the person and, at their worst, can block the development of empathy and rapport. If you must ask questions, make them short and open-ended. Questions can be useful and effective if used in moderation and if you don't get distracted into asking for irrelevant details. Following are some questions and phrases that can be helpful if they are used along with effective paraphrasing and reflecting:

Can you tell me more?
I don't think I understand. Can you go over that again?
Please go on.
Can you help me understand how you were feeling?
I don't think I am following you. Can you repeat that?
How were you feeling then?

Note that all of these questions are directed at helping you, the counselor, better understand the client and how he or she was feeling.

(2) Develop a Focus

After you have a good working relationship and a reasonable idea of what is bothering the student (and by the way, this won't always happen), it is time to help the student sort out and focus on the central issues. Often, students who seek counseling are overwhelmed by thoughts and emotions so that they can't really make any sense out of what is happening to them. A person serving as a counselor can help the student understand and identify the main issues at hand. Consider the example of Janet:

Janet comes to her English professor crying, and tells him that she feels depressed all of the time and can't get any work done. She reports that her friends are getting tired of her being down so much and are starting to avoid her. As her teacher talks with her, he begins to understand that much of Janet's sadness and depression is related to the loss of her mother. Her sadness centers around feeling alone and missing the closeness that she and her mother shared. She had a very close relationship with her mother (they talked on the phone several times a week) and she hasn't really had that kind of support since her mother died. Over the summer she was with the rest of her family and felt supported at home, but since coming back to school she hasn't had anybody with whom she can really talk.

The focus of counseling in this situation would probably be Janet's feelings about losing her mother, her loneliness for someone to support her, and her need to become more independent and function with the support of other friends.

Another illustration of developing a focus in counseling follows:

Eric is a new college student. He is twenty-eight and is just going back to college. He has been in the army for six years and finally decided that he wants to go to school to become an engineer. By November of his first semester he is overwhelmed by the academic work of an engineering curriculum. He discusses the situation with his academic advisor, who notes that he seems very anxious. He reports that he hasn't been sleeping or eating well and he says that he just can't get all of the work done. He is thinking about leaving school and feels like a failure. His decision to come back to school was a hard one and now he feels like it was a mistake. As his advisor talks with Eric he realizes that Eric just doesn't know how to study or manage his time. He seems like a very bright student, and does not have other problems that are interfering with his academic progress. (Note that the advisor learns about his lack of other problems by asking some questions and actively listening to Eric.)

This case illustrates a situation where the focus of counseling might be on developing study and time-management skills. By responding to this student's feelings, and listening to what he was feeling, his advisor was able to help him realize that his study-skill deficits and study behavior were the basic problems. The beginning step and patient listening were very important in order to determine an appropriate focus for counseling.

Helping someone sort out the important issues isn't always easy. For one thing, the real issues are not always the ones that are presented or ones of which a student is aware. In some cases, the basic issues are not all that clear or are serious enough that a referral to a professional is necessary. Mark's situation, described below, illustrates a case where the issues are so complex that referral to a professional psychologist or psychiatrist is necessary:

> Mark was called in to talk with his residence hall advisor because the other students on the floor were worried about him. He was spending almost all of his time in his room and he often seemed very depressed. In the conversation with his residence advisor, he revealed the fact that he had been chronically depressed for a long time and that, as he put it, his family situation was really screwed up. He said that his father didn't love him and that both of his parents would just as soon not have to deal with him. He also expressed considerable self-hate and couldn't really believe that any of the students on his floor really liked him.

This is perhaps an extreme case, but it illustrates a situation where professional help is clearly needed. In this case, the resident advisor needs to make a referral.

(3) Contract to Counsel the Student or Refer Him or Her to a Professional

In all three of the previous examples, the faculty member or advisor reached a point early in the interaction where a decision had to be made about whether to continue or to make a referral. This decision should come as early as possible in the interaction. In other words, after the initial counseling is structured ("Yes, I have some time to talk to you about your feelings of sadness"), there is a decision point where the person taking on the counseling role must decide where to go next. This decision is not an easy one for a nonprofessional counselor, since it requires an assessment of the situation. In examples 1 and 2 in the previous section (Janet, the student who was depressed because she no longer had her mother to depend upon; and Eric, the twenty-eight-year-old new student who needed help with time management and study skills), the counselor made an assessment that he or she could be helpful and was willing to spend some time counseling the student. In example 3 (the case of Mark who was chronically depressed), the advisor decided that he couldn't counsel the student after he learned more about the situation.

In all three cases discussed, and as a general principle, the need for referral or the agreement to continue with counseling should be explicit. A contract of some sort needs to be agreed upon before proceeding. This may seem too formal for a few help sessions between a teacher or advisor and student, but an understanding at the beginning about what will and will not happen can save considerable misunderstanding later. The contract need only be an agreement between the parties involved about the general content and time involved. For example, with Janet, the English professor might say, "I can see that since you lost your mother you really need someone to be there for you. Why don't you and I spend a few hours trying to figure out how you can find the support you need. I would be willing to meet with you three times during the next month to discuss this. What do you think?" Or, the engineering advisor might say to Eric, "It sounds like you need to learn a lot more about how to study. Why don't you sign up for the time-management course being offered at the counseling center, and meet with me every other week to talk about how you can improve your study and organizational skills?"

The case of Mark, who needs to be referred, is more difficult. This whole process of referral will be dealt with later on in a chapter devoted to referral. The important thing to remember here is the fact that you, as the person who has begun counseling with someone, have the right to decide that you don't want to make an informal contract to continue counseling this person. Don't let your need to help or your sympathy for a student override your own best judgment. It will be much fairer for the student in the long run if you get him or her to a professional when the need is there.

(4) Establish Realistic Alternatives and Goals

Many novice counselors get impatient with step 1, where the major goal is to understand, express empathy, and get the story and feelings out. They want to do something, to get the student moving, to target some specific changes. Clearly there is a place for action in counseling, but only after you have sufficiently explored the problem and determined what kind of action really needs to happen. This can only come through discussion and mutual agreement by the student and counselor.

It is important to note here that there is not always a need in counseling for working on goals and alternatives. Sometimes all a student wants or needs is to be understood and heard. Many times when a student comes into my counseling office he or she already knows what needs to be done, but just doesn't have the courage or motivation to proceed. In reality, much of counseling is encouragement. As a counselor you encourage students to take risks and to develop themselves in positive ways. Usually the student needs help clarifying, articulating, and achieving goals, but sometimes just listening is enough. A young man came into my office a while ago trying to deal with the fact that a very close friend had committed suicide one year ago. The boy thought that he had dealt with the situation, but the loss of his girlfriend and an injury that took him out of his favorite sport had somehow caused him to feel deeply again the loss of his friend. He felt that he shouldn't be having these strong feelings and eventually broke down and sobbed as he explored his feelings. He really didn't have any specific goals that he needed to work on, although you could say that the goal established in a kind of unwritten way was to explore and express his feelings. He really just needed someone to understand what he was feeling and to help him feel okay about his sadness. The depression that he had been laboring under for several months lifted after this session and he was able to put energy into his classes again.

When you are dealing with students with whom goals need to be defined and discussed, remember that these goals should be somewhat specific. Wanting to be happier and feel less depressed are certainly reasonable goals, but they are a bit too vague to focus on in counseling. In a case where a student articulated these goals for counseling, you would need to help the student get more specific. If you have spent time listening and building rapport with the student, you will probably have some ideas about what the student might do to improve his or her situation. Let's say that a student, John, is unhappy and depressed because he is not studying, is getting pressure from his parents to be more serious about school, feels that he is just floating, can't get motivated, and is not sure he even wants to be in school. He is very unhappy and depressed because of these problems. What can he do? The first step in goal setting is to have a student identify some goals (changed behaviors, activities, etc.) that he thinks would improve his situation. In this case John listed the following:

1. Get motivated and be more successful academically.
2. Get his parents to stop pressuring him.
3. Work out more (exercise).
4. Ask some girls out.

A student should be asked to spend some time thinking about the goals, so it was not at all unreasonable to ask John to bring in a list of goals to a counseling session. In this case, after reviewing these goals a number of questions were raised by the counselor. First, does John really want to be in school? What is his academic/career goal? Since he is not certain about being in school, he probably doesn't really have a goal. This may be a factor that negatively affects his motivation and it may also precipitate some of the pressure from his parents. The goal to work out more may mean that he is generally apathetic and feels as if he needs to improve his general health, or it may mean that he wants to improve his appearance and be related to his desire to ask some girls out on dates. Wanting to ask some girls out probably means that he is not happy socially and that he may feel isolated and as if he is not where he should or wants to be with women.

So, John has a number of things to work on. Assume, for the time being, that a graduate advisor has talked with him a couple of times and concluded that although his problems and feelings are intense, he really just needs some help getting past a kind of developmental block. In a situation like this a student might have some more serious problems, but in this case we will assume that a faculty member or advisor can work with this young man. After more discussion, the following goals were agreed upon:

1. Make a clear decision about school—whether to stay and really try, or drop out and work.
2. Talk to his parents about his feelings of pressure and share his thinking about the decision as to whether to leave school.
3. In the meantime, no matter what the decision, work on health and physical fitness.
4. Get involved in career-choice and career-development activities.
5. Begin to ask some girls out on dates.

For each of these goals, then, the counselor and student need to generate alternatives. Take goal one. Here are some possible alternatives:

1. Stay in school until the end of the semester and begin to look for a job in some way career-related.
2. Withdraw from school immediately and go home.
3. Drop out, work, and attend night school.
4. Drop out, travel, and find out what the world is really like.
5. Stay in school and work on achieving the other goals so that school will be a more positive and useful experience.

It is often important to articulate clearly all of the possible choices in this kind of decision making. For one thing, it helps the student realize that he really does have choices and that he can evaluate the pros and cons of each choice. It also helps the student really face his feelings about actually making a choice. In this case it is also apt to precipitate a more useful, although perhaps tense, dialogue with his parents.

Setting goals and outlining alternatives, when appropriate, may take some time and effort. Some students are not used to the process of thinking and deciding for themselves. They may actually expect the person who is their counselor to make decisions for them or they may feel that, even if they do make a decision to do something, they can't actually do it. For example, a young woman who is lonely and afraid to make new friends may set this out as a goal and devise several alternatives and strategies to make changes, but her negative beliefs and fear may make her feel as if she doesn't have the power to carry out her alternatives. One of the main functions of the counselor in cases like this is to help empower the student to make and carry out personal decisions. This may require the counselor to help the student reformulate his or her thinking about situations and to provide a strong kind of power and persuasion.

In addition to understanding and empathy, persuasion and power are important aspects of a counseling relationship. The counselor must often persuade the student to try new behavior and to change faulty thinking and beliefs. A combination of understanding, encouragement, and persuasion is often necessary. Take the example of a student who has never been very sure of himself. His father is a very critical man and has always focused on his son's shortcomings and failings. The son grew up believing that he wasn't very competent and developed an overly cautious, conservative approach to most aspects of life. In college he is well liked and respected by his classmates, and several of his fraternity brothers have encouraged him to run for the presidency of his fraternity. He is afraid to become a candidate and is very confused about the situation. He would like to feel strong enough to compete in the election, but just can't seem to get up the courage to go ahead with it. He is so anxious about the situation that he seeks out his fraternity's advisor to talk over the situation. In this case, after gaining an understanding of the situation, the advisor realizes that the young man's beliefs about himself are irrational and that he really does have what it takes to be a leader of his fraternity. Counseling, in this case, will involve helping the student develop the courage to risk seeing himself differently. If the risk pays off, even if he doesn't win, he will probably learn a very valuable piece of information about himself that may have profound implications for his future. Understanding, persuasion, and encouragement will all be important factors.

Some attention to skills can also be helpful. In the above example, the student does not have some of the interpersonal skills that he thinks are important to run for his fraternity office. He may never have been in a similar situation because of his belief that he wasn't very competent, fostered by an overcritical father. The lack of skill could take the form of his being very nervous about making a required speech to the entire fraternity. Part of what the counselor does might be directed at helping him learn something about this kind of speech making and how to manage the attendant anxiety.

(5) Devise an Action Plan

After the counselor and student have set up goals and considered different options for achieving the goals, it is time to devise an action plan. In this stage of counseling the counselor becomes a kind of coach, helping the student carry out a plan that will bring him or her closer to the established goals. Think back for a moment to the case of John. He was the young man who came in for help because he was unhappy and depressed, not doing well in school because he wasn't motivated, and dealing with increasing pressure from his parents to do better in school. After talking with a graduate advisor and discussing counseling goals he came up with four goals. For the first goal, which was to make a clear decision about school, he and the advisor came up with the alternatives mentioned on p. 38.

After pondering these different alternatives for goal one, John decided that he wanted to salvage the semester and try to make progress in finding a career. He also considered alternatives for his other goals and decided that he needed to talk with his parents about his feelings of being pressured too much, and exercise regularly. He and the advisor also decided that now wasn't the time to also focus on his goal of having more dates. They decided that he would postpone that goal until they made progress on the others.

Hopefully, this review of John's case will help you see how the stage must be set for developing the action plan. John is now ready to establish some specific actions and behaviors that will lead him to accomplishing his goals. Another way of looking at this process might be to view the action plan as a listing of subgoals. I use the term *action plan* because it implies that a part of the work must be on the specific accomplishment for each subgoal. There are several things to consider when working with a student on an action plan:

1. Create small steps so that the student has a good chance of success.
2. Reinforce and encourage success.
3. Plan for some failures.

4. Practice needed new verbal and other skills when necessary (i.e., rehearse conversations, practice taking notes, practice relaxation techniques).
5. Use available resources.
6. Set a timetable, but be flexible.

The key to much positive change and improvement is in being creative about setting steps toward a larger goal. For example, one of John's goals is to salvage the semester and begin the process of finding a career goal. What small action steps might be taken in pursuit of this goal? John and his advisor might decide that the first step would be to assess his status in each course. This might involve talking to each teacher and setting up a long-range study schedule for the rest of the term. After the long-range schedule is set, John can plan out his weekly schedule to include adequate study time, but the first step is to talk with the professors and map out his academic obligations for the rest of the term.

To reinforce and encourage John, the advisor might ask him to check in with her after he talks with the first two teachers so that she can provide some reinforcement and help if he has any problems. She might also ask him to write out his semester plan and let her take a look at it. She should also congratulate him on his decision and courage in confronting a difficult problem. In addition to the counselor's reinforcement, John will also feel good about himself for confronting his problem, and will probably be encouraged to continue. Often, making a start is the most important step in the counseling process. The use of reinforcement and encouragement can be a bit paradoxical in counseling, because the general goal of counseling is to help a student become self-sufficient and independent, not to rely upon another person for support. This kind of encouragement and reinforcement allows the student to develop confidence, skills, and to eventually learn how to become more self-sufficient.

Practice and skill building may be necessary before the first action steps can be taken. John may be so afraid of talking with his professors that he just won't go to see them. He may imagine that they won't be interested in talking with him or that they will judge him harshly because he isn't doing well. His counselor may need to help him plan what he wants to say and how he might react if he gets any negative reactions (a clear possibility). Role playing—a rehearsal with the counselor playing one of the parts (in this case the part of the professor)—can be very helpful to a student who is unsure of how or what to say. This is one instance where the counselor *can* offer advice and direct assistance.

Most college campuses offer a number of resources in terms of formal offices and informal contacts that can be very helpful to students. In John's case, working through the career counseling office can help him with his career direction goal. College career counseling offices have interest and personality tests available, as well as career materials and computer guidance systems. Faculty and staff who are working in particular careers can also help, as can offices that coordinate volunteer service. The advisor, in this instance, would serve as a moderator and facilitator in this area.

Setting a timetable is one of the most difficult parts of an action plan. The counselor must respect the student's readiness, yet he or she needs to provide some impetus to get the student started. Many times there is considerable reticence and fear on the student's part. The best approach is to involve the student in setting a timetable and checking in with progress periodically. This provides some impetus to accomplish, and also allows the counselor to monitor progress and to deal with unexpected difficulties and circumstances as needed. Committing the timetable to writing in some form of contract can be helpful. Research has shown that when people commit themselves in writing they are more likely to carry through with their commitment. Be careful about trying to accomplish too many action steps at one time. For example, in this case the advisor was wise not to attempt to deal with the dating goal along with everything else. Often, the counselor and student must do some prioritizing to decide where to start.

(6) End Counseling and Evaluate

I alluded to the problem of dependence when I discussed the paradox of providing considerable support and encouragement, and at the same time working toward more self-sufficiency and independence. As a counselor, you must find the right time to end your counseling relationship when the student has made some progress and can go off and continue to use what he or she has learned in counseling. Sometimes counselors and students have a tendency to continue too long because they are both gratified by the relationship and the progress being made. Continuing too long is also impractical from a time standpoint for the counselor and can be harmful to the student if it gives the message that you, as the counselor, don't trust the student enough to go out on his or her own.

A gradual termination of counseling can be helpful. Some faculty members and others serving as counselors maintain a kind of as-needed relationship with students, seeing them periodically to check on their progress. This system can work well if it is used judiciously. My own preference is for a kind of formal ending. In reality, the counseling relationship should be established with an ending in mind. Professionals often discuss "termination" issues when they finish counseling someone. These issues have to do with the difficulty both clients and counselors have in saying good-bye. A counseling relationship, by definition, is a close one that brings two people together to discuss very personal material. It is not unusual for both parties to develop affectionate feelings and to enjoy their contacts. This relationship sometimes reminds clients and counselors of their child-parent or parent-child relationships and can bring up feelings about those past relationships. All of this can work to make ending the relationship difficult. Two things can help during the final few sessions. First, the counselor should remind the student that they will only be seeing each other once or twice more. This will allow both parties to begin to process their feelings and to prepare for the termination. Second, the counselor should encourage the student to talk about feelings and fears about going out on his or her own. The student may need to be encouraged to realize that he or she is strong enough and has the tools to deal with problems. The counselor and student can also discuss how the student might cope if he or she feels overwhelmed or seems to have trouble continuing progress.

This entire discussion, with all of the steps and advice, may seem a bit too involved for much of the short-term counseling that faculty and other staff might do with students. In reality, you will often not be able to go through all of these desired procedures. I have presented them in the hope that they will help you understand a kind of basic model. Naturally, they may have to be modified according to individual student needs.

Some of the steps do seem especially crucial to me and I would recommend not bypassing them if at all possible. First, you must establish rapport and listen to what a student is saying. No matter how pressed you are for time, jumping in immediately with a solution, even if it seems most efficient, will not help in the long run. Second, make certain that you and the client have some agreement on process and goals. That is, you should both agree that you will provide some counseling toward some specified goals. Lastly, I urge you to gain familiarity with the mental health and other important resources on your campus. If you enter into even informal and apparently manageable counseling relationships, you will often find more complex and difficult problems under the surface. Be prepared to make referrals and to deal with this likelihood. It also helps to have a contact in the counseling center or some other comparable agency with someone whom you can use as a consultant when necessary. There is certainly no need to feel unsuccessful if a referral is necessary. If you help a student begin to deal with some more serious problem that is very likely to interfere with his or her life later on, you are doing that student a great service.

3

Personality

As you talk with students and get to know them, you begin to form opinions about how they see themselves and the world, and about how they interact with others. The better you understand these perceiving, thinking, and interactional processes, the easier it is for you to empathize with and understand a student. A particular model or structure for viewing these processes (sometimes called personality) can improve your observational abilities and help you come to a better understanding of the student and his or her internal world.

I must admit that I am somewhat dubious about writing a short chapter on personality. After all, there are dozens of different personality theories, and many volumes written attempting to explain a very complicated subject. In fact, there are some psychologists who don't even believe that a "personality" exists. They contend that we behave mostly because of the way we learn to respond to various stimuli. My strategy to avoid hopeless oversimplification will be to select one particular personality system that I believe is quite useful in understanding college students. Hopefully, my description of this theory, with examples related to some typical college student problems, will be helpful.

Jung's Theory of Type

Part of Carl Jung's theory of personality, which has been operationalized in the Myers-Briggs Type Inventory (MBTI) uses a typology to describe personality. According to this theory, four main attitudes and functions govern how we interact with the world and with each other, and each of us has a *preference* for how we operate within each attitude or function. Preference means the preferred way of operating; and does not mean that one does not, or cannot, use abilities and behaviors in the opposite preference. Thus, by determining your preference within each of the four areas, you have one kind of description of your personality; and by putting the four preferences together you have your personality "type." If you have access to the MBTI (through a counselor or psychologist) you may want to take the inventory to help you assess your own preferences. The inventory is not necessary for you to use this chapter, however. The theory is described here in some detail, and you will have a chance to assess your own preferences directly. This should serve as a good introduction to the theory and use of the system with students. A section on some of the specific applications to learning styles and some common college student problems will also help you learn to use this particular system in your thinking about student personality.

Basic Description of Attitudes and Functions

Read through the following description carefully. As you learn about the preferences within the attitudes and functions, think about where you fall for each preference. Later you will be asked to decide about your own preference in each area.

1. General Attitude toward the World

Extroversion—Introversion

Extroverts are outer-directed. They get their primary stimulation from the environment. *Introverts* are inner-directed. They are more concerned with their own inner world of thoughts and ideas. Extroverts like conversation, and are friendly, easy to know, and expressive. They are action-oriented and seldom spend time in reflection. Introverts are private, reserved, and hard to know. They usually have only a few close friends and spend considerable time thinking and processing their experiences internally. *Remember that no one is all extrovert or all introvert,* but, according to the theory, we do all prefer one attitude over the other.

Example:

Sharon, an introvert, has a free Friday evening. She has been asked to go to a large party at a friend of a friend's. She also received a call from an old friend who wants to get together and catch up. She chooses dinner with the old friend because she likes the idea of a small intimate interaction. An extrovert has the same options. He invites the old friend to come to the party with him because he doesn't want to miss the stimulation of all the people at the party.

2. Ways of Perceiving and Taking in Information

Sensing—Intuition

People with a preference for the sensing function take in information directly through the five senses. People who prefer intuition take in information more indirectly and tend to filter their perception through past experiences and expectations. *Sensors* are practical, observant, and tend to see things in smaller parts. They usually don't like theory and abstraction, and are usually literal minded. They like facts and details, and are often happy with the status quo. *Intuiters* are often dreamers and theorizers. They like change, variety, and can be impractical. They like fitting things together and often don't notice individual parts. They are imaginative, innovative, and often focus on the future.

Example:

Two people, one a strong sensor and one a strong perceiver, go to an art gallery and view a particularly famous painting. They discuss it afterwards. The sensor remembers the colors, the texture, the frame, and the details of the content. The intuiter hardly remembers the actual painting, but goes on to describe in great detail the fantasy and reactions that the painting caused in him.

3. Ways of Judging and Making Decisions

Thinking—Feeling

People who prefer *thinking* are logical and analytical. They decide things by thinking and they can be objective and impersonal, but may have trouble empathizing with other people's feelings. Those who prefer *feeling* are emotional, understanding, warm, and spontaneous. They can be overly sensitive and easily have their feelings hurt. They see things from personal, value perspectives, and they have trouble being analytic and objective.

Example:

Two people are arguing about an important issue. One is a feeler and one a thinker. The thinker has a number of facts to back up her position and quotes statistics to show that she is correct. The feeler argues passionately that she disagrees, but she doesn't have many facts or arguments to back up her position. She tends to be overwhelmed in arguments and gets carried away by her emotions.

4. Preferred Life-style and Ways of Interacting with the World

Judgment—Perception

Those who prefer *judging* like an organized, orderly approach to life. They like clear limits and parameters, and they like to have their lives under their own control. They don't like changes. People who prefer *perceiving* like to be spontaneous and to take life as it comes. They emphasize perception or interaction with the world, rather than judging or controlling it. They prefer to be able to be flexible, and tend to be disorganized and do things at the last minute.

Example:

Two people, one a strong judger and one a strong perceiver, get up on a free Saturday morning. The judger prefers to have the day planned out, to know what he is going to do when, and doesn't want to have to change his plans. The perceiver doesn't want to make plans. She wants to wake up and see what she feels like doing, to be spontaneous.

Now it is time to decide upon your own preferences. According to the theory you must place yourself in either one or the other category. However, you can indicate the strength of the preference. Remember, you are rating your preference for one dimension over the other. That doesn't mean that you don't also have abilities and behaviors from the opposite preference. For example, if you rate yourself as more feeling than thinking, that doesn't mean that you never use thinking in your judgments. It does mean that you *prefer* to use feeling rather than thinking. Rating yourself on these dimensions may be difficult. Make a strong effort to be honest and not to rate yourself as you would like to be, rather than as how you really are. If you have a close friend who will take a few minutes to read the dimensions and then discuss your preferences with you, that would be a good way to cross-check your own perceptions of yourself.

Rate your preference and the strength of these preferences. Use the following examples as a guide.

Extroversion/Introversion

Example:

Janice is pretty good at interacting with people. She can talk with strangers at parties and has a number of friends. However, she is a private person in many ways and doesn't confide in people easily. She also likes to spend time alone, and prefers to socialize with a few close friends, even though she enjoys a large and wild party occasionally.

Janice has some extroverted characteristics, but her basic preference seems to be toward introversion. She might be rated as a "moderate" introvert. (Be careful not to be fooled by behavior and abilities in the area. They don't necessarily reflect your preference.)

Sensing/Intuition

Example:

Ted has always been a great athlete. He loves the outdoors and the feel of playing sports. He is also an outdoorsman and enjoys hiking, camping, and swimming. He is a very keen observer and can remember many details of what he sees. He is also very realistic and is very impatient with dreamers and people who want to discuss things too long. He is known as a doer. In school he hated anything that was too theoretical and abstract.

Ted would appear to be a very strong sensor. He seems to perceive things directly through his senses and he dislikes anything that is not realistic and down-to-earth. He would probably be rated as a very strong sensor.

Thinking/Feeling

Example:

Marjorie works as a physical therapist. She loves her work, although she often gets very emotionally involved with her patients. She is very sensitive and is also very good at counseling them and helping them deal with the psychological aspects of their recovery. Although she is sensitive and good at understanding the feeling of her patients, she doesn't lose control of her emotions and she can be objective and thoughtful at times.

Marjorie prefers feeling in her interactions, but because she also uses thinking and objectivity at times, she is probably a "strong" and not a "very strong" feeler.

Judging/Perceiving

Example:

Juan is a very good student. He is well organized and has a very tight time-management plan. His desk is always very orderly and there is a place for everything. His friends see him as a very organized person. However, they don't like the fact that he can never seem to change his plan or act spontaneously.

It is fairly obvious that Juan is a "very strong" judger. Everything in his life is orderly and he has trouble when he cannot control aspects of his life.

After you have assessed your own preference in each area take some time to examine your four preferences. Write them down so that you can think about how they interact with each other. For example if you are an extrovert who prefers sensing and thinking you are probably very action and fact-oriented. However, you may get very impatient with people who want to consider alternatives and put facts into some kind of larger theory. Or, if you are an introvert and a feeler, you probably get your feelings hurt a lot, but people may not understand the hurt since you probably don't tell them about it very often. The combinations and relationships of preferences are complex and beyond the scope of this discussion. Without further study of the system or some other personality system, your goal should be to look for some *basic* personality structures that seem to be important to the problems and difficulties that your students are experiencing.

Although I will refer to personality in my discussion of specific college student problems in the remaining chapters, it will be helpful, I think, to examine briefly the implications of personality type to learning and to discuss some specific cases that illustrate the importance of personality type.

Personality and Learning

Since the major function of a college or university is to teach students, a college student counselor must always be aware of the teaching and learning process. Many college student problems are strongly related to learning difficulties. Unfortunately, most of our colleges and universities don't take into account the fact that students have different learning styles. Professors typically treat all students the same, and teaching methods often favor certain learning styles.

Take, for example, a student who is a strong sensor on the MBTI. This person is fact-oriented and makes sense out of what he learns by understanding facts and probably the application or use of facts. He will undoubtedly have trouble in a course that is very theoretical. Let's say that he takes a history course and the professor emphasizes several different theories about the political developments in the early twentieth century. This student will have to make sense out of these theories by understanding some facts, specifics, and applications. If the professor emphasizes theory and asks for abstract comparisons of several different theories, this student will have a difficult time. If, on the other hand, another history professor teaches the same course and is primarily interested in facts and specifics, and tends to see events and specific influences as important, a student who has a strong preference for intuition will have a terribly difficult time. Learning a great number of facts and specifics will be very hard unless the student can somehow fit them all together into some kind of theory or organized set of relationships.

In many courses, including history, both of the above approaches to learning can be helpful; however, in some classes a great deal of frustration is generated when the teaching methods do not accommodate a variety of learning styles. Also, some courses by their very nature are extremely theoretical or extremely fact-oriented. A counselor may have to help a student understand that his or her personality makes studying a specific course or curriculum very difficult. I am reminded of a common occurrence regarding engineering students. Often a freshman engineering student will show up in my office frustrated about progress in engineering. They have usually been very good with electrical or mechanical things while growing up, and parents and others assumed that they would make wonderful engineers. Unfortunately, their talents were with putting electrical or mechanical devices together, a basically sensing orientation. They enjoyed figuring out specific parts and functions and fitting them together. They discover quickly, however, that studying engineering means understanding calculus, physics, and other disciplines that are very theoretical. Their learning styles and personalities often do not really match what is required to study engineering.

Another important preference with regard to learning style is the perceiving-judging preference. You will recall that someone who prefers perceiving tends to be a good reactor and isn't particularly comfortable with structure and organization. The judger, on the other hand, likes to be organized, to fit things into structures, and to organize the world to his own liking. If a student who is a strong perceiver takes a course in which the professor tends to give lectures that are not organized, and diverge in many different directions, that student will have a difficult time making sense out of the lectures and organizing the material. A judger, on the other hand, may be able to rise to the challenge and come out of the lectures with notes that do make sense out of what the professor has said. The judger will be able to assess how the material fits into the structure of the course and with the other materials used for the course.

In counseling students with these kinds of learning style problems and mismatches, the counselor often finds him- or herself trying to help students develop their ability to use an attitude or method of perceiving or judging that is not their natural preference. If you can assess students' preferences, and help them understand how their learning style is getting in the way, you will have a much better chance of achieving some growth and helping them make helpful modifications.

Knowledge of personality can also be useful in really understanding a student's behavior. The young woman who just can't get anything out of lectures and who takes terrible notes, is not necessarily a poor student or lazy or unmotivated. She may just not have the natural organizational skills to bring information together into some kind of understandable structure. I should mention here that, just as in the first example, the opposite learning style can also be problematic. The student who is too rigidly organized and structured may have difficulty responding to a question or an idea that is beyond his or her organizational confines. He or she may have difficulty with requirements to transfer knowledge from one set of circumstances to another. Another dimension, the sensing/intuition preference, may also enter in here. The judger, with sensing as a preference may have good organization and structure, but have difficulty connecting facts and specifics to a larger theory.

Personality Preference Case Examples

In addition to learning style, personality preferences can play a major role in many different kinds of student problems. The following three case studies illustrate this point:

Case 1

Alex came in to see his history teacher because he failed the midterm exam. Because he is a freshman, the instructor thought that he might just not know how to study. However, after talking with him for a few minutes, the instructor realized that Alex was very unhappy at college and that he was failing most of his courses. This didn't make sense in terms of his ability, since he had SAT scores in the top 10 percent of students in his freshman class.

As Alex talked the portrait of a young man who was very lonely and unable to make friends emerged. Alex was a strong introvert and just didn't know how to become friends with other students in his dorm. He grew up in the same neighborhood, and had two or three boyhood friends with whom he had been very close all through school. He had never been very social, but it didn't bother him because he had his close buddies to hang out with. He had hoped to make friends with his roommate, but it turned out that his roommate had many other friends and was gone from the room most of the time.

Alex had not had great self-confidence as a kid, and was beginning to feel very badly about himself, and was feeling that he was very inferior to those around him. He was thinking about dropping out of school and reported that his parents were very worried about him. He was so upset by all this that he just wasn't able to concentrate and study, even though he had done quite well in high school.

This case is an excellent example of a developmental problem that becomes a crisis. Alex had never really confronted his introversion and poor social skills, and being in a new environment and reaching an age when he needed to develop new friendships forced him to confront this in himself. As with many introverts, Alex always wished that he could be more social and has always been envious of those who can interact easily with others. He had never seen any strengths in being introverted and his current situation makes him feel very inferior as an introvert.

One of the major tasks of a counselor in this kind of case is to help a person come to grips with his or her own pluses and minuses. Alex must accept the fact that he is more introverted than extroverted and learn to appreciate the good parts of this preference. This will be much easier if he learns how to form friendships and realizes that even introverts can make and develop new friendships. Encouragement and some help in figuring out how to approach people he wants to get to know will help a lot in this situation. The counselor will need to empathize and understand his pain, yet also help him realize that he is facing some new challenges that he can learn to confront.

Case 2

Sarah is a woman in her early forties who is coming back to school after raising a family. She has become president of the returning adult student organization and is having problems with her leadership style. Other members of the executive committee find her abrasive and too aggressive. She comes for help to the assistant dean who advises the organization.

It turns out that she has always had a number of conflicts with others who have frequently told her that she is too pushy and aggressive and that she isn't very sensitive. This has been a very difficult thing with which to deal and she remembers being really hurt as a teenager when she was accused of being unfeminine and too masculine. Fortunately, she married a man who appreciates her and likes the fact that she is strong and forceful, but this incident has made her angry and she really wants to figure out why this kind of conflict keeps on occurring in her life.

The advisor soon realizes that one of the major problems she has encountered is the fact that she has a strong personality preference for thinking rather than feeling. In some ways this goes against the stereotype of soft, understanding women that she grew up with. Her thinking preference seems to make her come on very strong in discussions, often with very good and sound arguments; however, because she is not very much in touch with her affective or feeling side, she has trouble understanding why others are sometimes hurt and angry at her. Her husband is also a strong thinker, so she hasn't really had to confront that issue with him. They tend to argue strongly with each other, but neither of them usually gets his or her feelings hurt.

The strategy for helping Sarah will probably involve getting her to understand better how her strong thinking process overwhelms her ability to respond to emotion and to be sensitive to other people's emotions. She may have used her strong thinking abilities to defend against emotion in the past, perhaps to avoid being hurt or to cope with a difficult family situation. In any case, a major goal of counseling will be to help her develop her emotional side, and to learn how to be more sensitive to the feelings of others and to her own feelings.

Case 3

Patrick came in to the college chaplain's office looking very disturbed. He had a hard time getting his problem out, but he finally blurted out the fear that he might be gay. He told the chaplain that he had sex with a guy in his dormitory and that he was feeling very anxious and afraid. He had not intended to have sex with this person, but they had been out drinking and had come back to the other fellow's room to watch TV. Patrick admitted that he sometimes thought about having sex with men, but he always thought that those were just fantasies and not reality. Now it was reality and he didn't know how to deal with it.

Although dealing with homosexuality in our culture is traumatic in itself, the chaplain learned that much of what was bothering Patrick was having to deal with this unexpected and unpredictable event. Patrick was a very organized person and he had his life mapped out. He was going to go to medical school, become an ophthalmologist, then get married and have two children. He pictured himself in an idyllic house with a large lawn and lots of room for his children to play. Dealing with the possibility of being gay was not something that he planned on.

The chaplain wisely tried to get him to calm down and not interpret this one event as something that would necessarily change his entire life-style. Much of his panic was caused by the surprise and necessity of dealing with an unexpected event. The chaplain realized that he was a strong judger and that the loss of control and the necessity of dealing with something very significant and unexpected was a significant part of his problem.

The chaplain, in this case, referred Patrick to the campus counseling center where he saw a psychologist and attempted to deal with his sexual orientation. Although he wasn't really able to decide for certain about his sexual preferences and orientation, he did learn to accept the possibility that he might have to adapt to a life-style very different from the one that he had planned.

In each of these examples I have attempted to show how the student's personality, defined in terms of the MBTI preferences, can play a very significant role in problem situations. An understanding of the role of personality in learning and in general student problems will help you understand some of the whys and hows of a student's behavior as well as providing some structure and perhaps direction for needed growth and development. Even if you cannot assess the role of personality in a particular student's concerns, it may be helpful to think about and even discuss the problem in terms of personality.

4

Academic Success

Nothing is more important for most students than the achievement of academic success. Grades are clearly the most important measure of academic success and are seen by most students as the most important determinant of future life success. This perception may or may not be true, but it certainly exists; and anyone taking on the role of counselor to college students must confront problems related to academic success. Faculty members, in particular, are very likely to encounter students who are not doing well in their classes and who are very concerned about their grades.

As you will see throughout this book, many different kinds of problems and developmental blocks can be part of a student's grade difficulties. The most important part of a counselor's job in this arena is to help a student sort out his or her problems and make an assessment of what really is the cause of poor grades and academic performance. Many students tend to put the blame on poor study skills, and sometimes this is the central problem. A faculty member, advisor, or anyone else taking on a counseling role, however, should not accept "study skills" as the problem without adequate exploration. Often poor study skills are just part of a student's difficulties. As a counselor you may or may not want to work with the student on personal problems that are interfering with good academic performance. You may just want to contract with the student to help with some specific study skills.

In this chapter guidelines are presented for helping students with study-related problems in three general areas: (1) motivation, (2) time management, and (3) study skills. Many campuses have excellent resources for help in these areas, so you may or may not choose to get involved as a counselor. Keep in mind, however, that, as a trusted counselor and someone who has some understanding of a particular person, you may have the best opportunity to provide help. Just referring a student to a study skills class can be helpful, but there is no substitute for the personal attention and support that an individual can provide.

(1) Motivation

A student's motivation can be related to, and affected by, all kinds of personal and developmental factors. Although the causes of poor motivation can be complicated and difficult to identify, it is crucial that they be dealt with at the onset. There is no real point in discussing better time management or improved study skills if the student is not really motivated. The change in behavior required to improve academic performance requires resolve and motivation. Several factors should be considered in attempting to deal with student motivation problems. First, the commitment to being in college is important. Many students of traditional age move into college just because it seems like the next step, and they really have no particular reason for being in school. Many of these students would be much better off out of school for a while until they have some sense that they want to go to college. Often parents have trouble dealing with the alternative of leaving school and sometimes students pick up fears from them that if they don't attend college now they never will. It may be very helpful for a counselor to confront a student with this kind of motivation problem and talk about the alternative of leaving school and doing something else.

Related to the problem of not really wanting to be in school is the difficulty of not really having any goals. Sometimes what is needed for improving motivation is career counseling and help with establishing career and life goals. The next chapter covers career choice and describes an effective career development process. A student's level of academic values can also play a significant role in motivation. Students from families with high academic values, who have already learned to study and to value academic work, have a much easier time than those from families where not as much value was placed on studying and learning. Often the latter come to college primarily to improve their economic status and have trouble seeing how the study of poetry in English 101 has anything to do with becoming a lawyer. A counselor has limited ability to change this kind of value system, but it may be possible to help these students develop a strategy to deal with courses that seem totally irrelevant to them.

Motivation can also be strongly affected by a student's peer group and residence location. Students who live with roommates who do not study and who do not value learning often have difficulty keeping their own motivation up. If roommates go out to party most evenings it will be pretty difficult for an individual to resist the peer pressure to join them. Also, study environments for campus and off-campus residences vary a great deal. Students often don't realize how strong the effect of their peer group is on their motivation, and it can be very helpful to discuss this influence and possible ways to change environments if that would improve the student's personal academic climate.

(2) Time Management

In my view the greatest single factor determining academic success is time management. In order to manage time effectively a student must have his or her life well organized, have some clearly defined goals and priorities, and have a realistic sense of personal needs and priorities. The college environment contains many elements that make good time management difficult. The primary challenge is in effectively organizing and allocating time to a great number of academic and other activities. For many traditional-age college students this is a new challenge and one that offers perhaps too many choices and alternatives. Personal and academic needs often conflict. A bull session at 2:00 A.M. about dreams for the future may be hard to pass up in favor of getting to bed when one has a test the next day. For older than average students effective time management is an absolute necessity. For many of them there is literally not a spare minute in their busy schedules. Families, jobs, and personal time all compete with school related activities.

Personality factors are important in time management. Being organized and structured comes more naturally for some people. If you recall the judging dimension on the MBTI (personality system discussed in chapter 3) people have preferences for how they like to deal with the external environment. Some people prefer to organize and structure the environment and like to have control over their environment. Others like to react and respond, and prefer less control and more spontaneity. Obviously, the people who prefer reacting and less control have a harder time managing and organizing their time. These personality differences are important to note when trying to help a student develop a personal time management plan. People who don't like structure and find it confining, need to find ways to manage time that still allows them flexibility.

Two types of time scheduling are crucial for college students: semester-long planning and weekly planning. Every student needs a calendar for each semester or quarter that shows when major papers, tests, and other assignments are due. This schedule should also include major personal commitments so that the student can plan the time necessary for each major activity. A periodic review and updating of this calendar is an excellent idea.

Weekly planning requires a system that allows a student to accomplish specific tasks within deadlines. Two general systems seem to work best: a weekly schedule-by-the-hour or a list system with things to do generated at the beginning of every day. The weekly schedule allows for an overview of weekly responsibilities and provides a fairly tight structure as well, enabling a student to plan personal and academic activities. This type of schedule may be just too restricting for some students. The alternate list system allows more flexibility and it allows for daily changes and reordering of priorities. Although many people manage this kind of listing system in their head, a written list is essential for students developing their time-management system. The list of things to do can also contain some kind of priority designator: perhaps the numbers one, two, or three to designate the level of priority.

The counselor's role in teaching time management is twofold: first, to assist the student in developing an effective system; and second, to help the student learn how to use it successfully. Often, just the process of focusing attention on time management is helpful. Students realize how much time they are wasting and develop a sense of time as a commodity that needs to be managed. Various blocks to using time management also often arise for some students. The counselor's role becomes that of a kind of motivator and reinforcer. It may be helpful to have the student check back weekly for a bit to report on his or her time-management progress. Usually when a student can't seem to get a system going, many other factors such as poor motivation, bad study environments, or lack of assertiveness (inability to say no to requests taking the student away from studying) are operational.

The question of balance must also be raised and confronted when one is learning how to manage time. A student's academic goals have to be balanced with personal needs. Students often fool themselves into thinking that they don't have time for exercise, regular meals, or healthy relationships because all of their time must be devoted to studying. It is crucial for them to consider their personal needs when setting up any kind of time-management plan. Study efficiency and the ability to concentrate come only with a proper balance. A frequently used "wellness" system includes six important life areas: emotional, intellectual, social, physical, spiritual, and career. Students must consider their needs in all of these life areas when developing a time-management schedule. Sleep, nutrition, and exercise are all important parts of the physical dimension. These areas are particularly likely to be ignored by college students. A counselor has limited influence in this area, since the environment often encourages poor nutrition and erratic sleeping habits. Inclusion of these needs in a time management plan can, however, help a student remember them and devote time to them.

(3) Study Skills

Once a student learns to manage time, has a reasonably clear set of goals, and is not distracted by personal problems, he or she is ready to study. However, many students arrive at a college or university without the necessary study skills. Many schools offer considerable assistance in this area and have special offices and programs. As a faculty member or other counselor you may only need to encourage participation and help reinforce positive behavior. On the other hand you personally may be in a position to help a student confront and try to improve study skill behaviors. For purposes of this discussion these skills are divided into four general areas: (1) reading, (2) writing, (3) classroom behavior, and (4) study/concentration.

The first step, and no easy one, is to help a student assess which study skills areas need attention. The best way to accomplish this assessment is through a careful discussion with the student of the different areas and inspection of a sample of his or her work. Discussion with faculty members who have the student in class can also provide valuable information. The following discussion of each area should help you work with students on the assessment process and with planning for improvement strategies.

Reading

There are several important reading skills. These include speed and flexibility, comprehension, vocabulary, and identifying main points. The key to reading quickly is taking in phrases rather than single words. Flexibility, of course, allows different speeds for different kinds of material. If a formal reading and comprehension test is not available through a campus testing or study skills office, you can give a rough test to students by asking them to read some material for a few minutes and then counting the words. Any student who cannot read material at several hundred words per minute needs some kind of speed-reading course or program.

Good comprehension requires a student to understand and use previewing, skimming, and scanning. Previewing involves familiarization with material prior to reading so that each book's organization and general approach to its subject are understood. Skimming is used to look for main ideas and topics and is often done prior to reading a chapter to uncover the main topics and ideas prior to actual reading. Scanning is a rapid search of the material for specific detail, such as important dates or specific events or phenomena. Later, in the section on studying, I will describe a widely used system called the SQ3R system that helps students systematically use different reading and comprehension skills in studying.

In much of the reading college students do, they must identify main points and supporting evidence. Many students are unable to sort out the main points. Understanding and identifying introductory and thesis statements are crucial. Learning to list and identify the supporting points and recognizing summaries and conclusions is also important. In many textbooks this process is made easier by headings, subheadings, and summaries. Although it is anathema to many students, one sure way of learning to identify main points and levels of information is to outline material. Granted, students don't have time to outline all the material they read, but learning how to outline material well will help students learn to order information as they read it. By giving students who have study problems an assignment to outline a particular assignment, you can learn a great deal about their ability to identify main points and you can help teach them the process of ordering information.

Critical thinking and the ability to evaluate the material read is critical. Often this kind of criticism and evaluation is what the professor asks for on an exam, and learning to critique what one reads as a kind of automatic process can be extremely useful. Most introductory English courses include some work on logic, argument, and criticism. You may need to review some of this material for students who have trouble making judgments about what they read. Following are some common types of faulty arguments that a student should be able to recognize:

1. Illogical comparisons.
2. Emotional appeal.
3. Slanted words and stereotypes.
4. Omission of material/incomplete information.
5. Poor logic—statements that do not follow.
6. Meaningless phrases/gobbledygook.
7. Poor balance.

Understanding the appropriate vocabulary requires a student to concentrate on learning new words introduced in any course. Of course, if the student doesn't understand other words he or she also needs to deal with them. One simple way to deal with words that one doesn't understand is to mark them in some way, and go back later and look them up. However, this can interfere with the flow of reading, particularly if there are many of these words. Sometimes reviewing new vocabulary prior to reading a particular chapter or part of a book is useful.

In textbooks key vocabulary words are often listed at the end of the chapter.

Writing

A faculty member, advisor, or someone else acting as a counselor to college students will certainly not have the time to teach a student to write well if the student has been unable to learn this set of skills in his or her prior educational experiences. Clearly, specialized courses, tutoring, writing labs, or other work are necessary for students with significant writing problems. There are a few key writing problems that even students who can write reasonably well might have with college courses. These problems usually involve producing term or research papers and writing essay exams. For research and term papers, the single biggest problem is one of time management. If you have time as a student's counselor you can ask him or her to produce a draft of a writing assignment several days ahead of the due date, as a way of forcing management of time so that a draft can be produced. The habit of producing a draft and getting someone else to read it and comment is also an invaluable technique for improving writing skills.

Successful research papers are seldom done in one or two days. The process of picking a topic and doing a particular kind of writing assignment may be new to students and particularly troublesome. They may have trouble with writing a critical essay, for example, if they have never really learned how to do that before. The best strategy in this kind of situation is for the student to see the instructor and get clarification. Since many students have trouble accessing faculty members in the college and university setting, the counselor's role is often one of helping the student learn to be assertive enough to make appointments and get what he or she needs.

Classroom Behavior

Many students underestimate the importance of their behavior in class. They frequently don't realize that what they do in class can have a rather strong influence on how much they learn and how well they do in terms of a grade. It can be helpful to persuade students to focus on three different kinds of behavior in class: (1) listening, (2) note taking, and (3) participation. To assess a student's classroom behavior a counselor probably needs to examine copies of their notes and also ask some questions about frequency of attendance and level of participation. Of course, getting to class regularly is crucial to the performance of any of the classroom behaviors mentioned above. Time management and motivation play an important role in classroom attendance, as do general attitudes about the usefulness of class. The counselor's role in helping a student assess and improve classroom behavior is one of guide and teacher, *not parent*. Nothing will doom success as much as parentlike injunctions about attending class.

Listening in class must be an *active* process. There is a strong tendency for students to sit passively and wait for knowledge to seep into their brains. Of course it doesn't happen that way. A student needs to be active mentally and to think about and truly follow what is being said. If students will learn to look for different components of a lecture, their attention level will be higher. Most lectures should have an introduction, a thesis or main argument, a discussion where the main ideas are supported, and a summary. Of course, not all lectures follow this format and not all lecturers are this well organized. Also, a student needs to be able to sort out the irrelevancies and sidetracks that really don't pertain much to the material at hand. Understanding whether the lecture is organized either inductively or deductively can also help a student's listening effectiveness. In deductive lectures, such as the one outlined above, the professor presents the main point and then gives illustrations and support. In inductive lectures the professor presents several factors or arguments and then draws his thesis or conclusion.

Everyone who has attended college has had the experience at one time or another of being in a lecture hall and suddenly realizing that they haven't been listening for the last twenty minutes. If this happens to a student very often he or she will miss significant amounts of material. The task of taking good notes, which will be described later, can help keep a student alert and focused. Preparation for the lecture by doing the reading beforehand can also help a great deal by allowing the student to be familiar with the material. A myriad of other factors can get in the way of a student's really listening to lectures.

These range all the way from lack of sleep to too much sexual activity. In counseling and teaching students in this area it is, once again, very important to explore the student's feelings and perceptions in order to assess just what is really interfering with good listening.

Note taking is much more important than most students realize. There are some very specific guidelines for taking good notes and it is fairly easy to review a student's notes to assess their level of note-taking effectiveness. Following are several important guidelines that you can give students:

1. Take legible notes, dated and labeled for each lecture.
2. Use your own words to restate what the lecturer says.
3. Highlight key words and define them.
4. Copy anything that is written on the blackboard.
5. Take notes in an outline format indicating levels of importance.
6. Edit and review notes after class sometime *during the same day*.
7. Keep a wide margin so that you will have room for comments when you edit and review.

Participating in class is very difficult for many students. Sometimes they just don't realize the advantage of being one of the active discussants. Active participation will help keep a student alert and involved. It often helps them gradewise, and they are more likely to keep up with the material and to think about it. It also fosters a positive attitude toward the class and allows a student to get his or her questions answered. Much of the hesitation that students have toward participating in class relates to feeling that their comments would be stupid and somehow demonstrate their ignorance. Some students have great trouble talking in any group situations. After discussing class participation with a student you may want to help him or her develop strategies for being more active. This may just involve some encouragement and better preparation, or it may require counseling to deal with the stress and anxiety. A later chapter will deal with stress and anxiety in general and will provide some suggestions for helping students deal with stressful situations like this one.

Study Concentration

What do you do as a counselor when a student says, "I just can't concentrate. My mind wanders every time I sit down to study"? I can report from experience that this is not an easy issue to deal with as a counselor. There are so many possible reasons for poor concentration that identifying them and intervening in some way is often extremely difficult. More often than not, problems with concentration are related to other life issues like poor motivation, lack of direction, depression, stress, relationship problems, loneliness, family problems, poor identity formation, and even substance or sexual abuse. The first step in counseling for this problem is to spend time trying to ascertain just what is interfering with the student's performance. This may or may not yield much information. Often the problems are so pervasive that students really don't understand or recognize them themselves. The most useful approach for faculty, advisors, and others is to spend time trying to determine causes and then decide whether a specific focus on concentration is appropriate.

Advice and information about how to improve concentration can be useful if work on the problem of concentration itself is called for. Also, improved study skills in general will help a student increase his or her ability to concentrate. Following are some suggestions that can be given to students for improving concentration:

1. Select one location for studying. This will develop a conditioned response so that study behavior will become automatic in this location.
2. Minimize possible distractions. Don't have magazines, newspapers, interesting tapes or CDs, radio, TV, interesting view out of windows, conversations, etc.
3. Have appropriate furniture, ventilation, lighting, etc.
4. Handle any organizational details before you sit down.
5. Turn off your phone or get an answering machine.
6. Take frequent short breaks if you start to daydream or fall asleep.
7. Try to set aside a regular time to study. Use time between classes during the day.
8. Keep a pad of paper to jot things down that come to you unrelated to studying—you can spend time on them later.
9. Try to finish any unfinished business before you start, e.g., make phone calls, shop, do the dishes.
10. Try to postpone socializing until after you complete your study period.

Certainly not every one of these suggestions works for every student. Some students study with the TV on and do well. Others are very sporadic and do well. However, for students not doing so well, all of these suggestions have merit. In counseling students in this whole area of study skills, it is difficult to avoid a kind of parental stance. A counselor can try to build motivation and reward positive behavior, but ultimately the student cannot be forced to change behavior and too heavy a hand can generate rebellious feelings very close to the surface, particularly in traditional-age students.

Three major methods are widely used for studying and learning classroom material. Some students find underlining or highlighting in their books helpful. Others outline material after reading each chapter, and still others use the SQ3R method, or some variation, as a systematic way to read and remember. The three methods are not mutually exclusive.

Underlining and highlighting is a time-honored tradition among students. Used textbooks are often filled with lines and yellow highlight. The basic challenge of this method is knowing how to pick out the important points to underline. One is restricted to what is actually in the book and there is no requirement to restate the material and the main points in one's own language. Also, for many students, studying consists of going back to study these underlinings a day or two before the test. I would classify this method as the least effective, primarily because there isn't enough processing of the material by the student. Outlining is far superior, but also very time consuming. Many students resist outlining because it takes too long. This may well be, but for some subjects and topics it may be worth the time. There are two important advantages: students are forced to determine levels of importance, and to work the material over in their minds and on paper. These both improve understanding and memory.

The SQ3R is a method that structures a student's approach to reading and studying material. The letters stand for: S = Survey, Q = Question, R = Read, R = Recite, and R = Review. The following instructions can be used for students:

(S) **Survey** the material (chapter, sections, etc.) and look for main points. Read the table of contents, chapter summaries, bold face type of every page, headings, italicized words, and summaries; and notice the order of presentation.

(Q) Turn the heading topics into **questions.** Authors sometimes pose questions in the beginning of the chapter. Keep these in mind as you read. This will keep you interested in the material and help you remember and understand the main points.

(R) **Read** to answer the questions you formed. Read the entire headed section immediately after you have formed the question. Read for the main ideas. This must be an active search for the answer to your questions, not just passive reading.

(R) After you have read a section, **recite** the answer to your questions in your own words and give an example if possible. Stop at the end of each section and try to recall what you have read. Strive to be a critical reader and read to answer questions—not only those formed by the headings, but also those that you have based on other information. Always complete the four steps (Survey, Question, Read, and Recite) with each subject heading.

(R) **Review** the material continuously. A systematic scheduling of a review of the material will aid in your review for exams. After you have read several chapters go back and review how the main points and subpoints are related. Attempt to integrate the material with what you have learned in class.

These study methods may not work well for certain courses or subjects, and students may be able to take certain parts of each of them and use them to the best advantage. The important thing for most students is to develop some kind of organized approach that allows them to process the material, make sense out of it, and remember it.

This chapter has offered a brief discussion of three important prerequisites to academic success: motivation, effective time management, and positive study skills. You have seen, I hope, the difficulty for a counselor in sorting out just what might be causing a student to perform poorly. Clearly, assessment and deciding where to focus the time you have available for counseling are crucial. With limited time the counselor needs to define just how much time he has to teach study skills, time management, and to deal with motivation problems. Referral to other help sources is often desirable, with perhaps some continuing contact for support and discussion.

5
Career Choice

$\mathbf{F}$inding a college major and setting a career goal are vexing problems for many college students. Few faculty members, advisors, or college counselors have not heard students describe intense anxiety and frustration about finding a career goal or life direction. Sometimes the lack of a career and academic goal is part of an overall sense of confusion and depression. Because having a career, particularly in contemporary society, is so important, students who are not able to settle on a visible and viable goal often feel defective, immature, and even hopeless. As counselor to one of these undecided students, your first task will be to respond to the anxiety and pressure that the student is feeling.

After you have responded to a student's anxiety you may want to help them get started on an active career development search. In this chapter I will outline a career choice process that I believe can be useful for most students who are involved in the career choice process. Also included will be a brief discussion of several career choice related topics that are important for counselors to consider. These include: career readiness, parental influence, college major and career choice, male/female and cross cultural issues, narrowing versus choosing, high-risk career goals, and graduate and professional school.

Career Readiness

Career choice comes at different times for different people. Some students come into college with very clear career goals, while others come in with absolutely no idea of what they want to do with their lives. Many different factors determine a student's readiness to choose a career. A student may just not have clearly enough defined interests to make any kind of choice, or he or she may have several strong competing interests. An identity may not have developed enough for him or her to be able to make such a significant commitment, or he or she may be so anxious about making a wrong choice that no choice at all can be made. A myriad of legitimate reasons exists to explain why a particular student may be "undecided" about a major and career. Unfortunately, our expectations and our college and university systems often demand a premature choice by certain times.

Most college students are required to choose a specific major by the end of their sophomore year. This doesn't mean that they have to choose a career by then; but usually, in order to choose the appropriate major, students want to have a career goal. There are exceptions. Some students resist thinking about the future and are determined just to study what really interests them. However, the need to choose a career direction eventually seems to manifest itself in nearly everyone's life. Parents who are footing the bill rightfully expect their children to have some direction; and many curricula, like engineering, must be set up so that a student begins to study a sequence of courses very early in the college years.

Even though a legitimate need for career choice and direction exists, I am still sympathetic to students who are forced to choose prematurely. One goal of any kind of career counseling should be to help a student pay attention to his or her own level of readiness. I don't mean that a student should not be active in trying to explore different options, but students, parents, advisors, and faculty members should try to view each student's career choice within the context of his or her own developmental pattern.

Readiness is perhaps an even more complex question for returning adult students. They have usually dealt with the career choice question before they return to school. The choice to return to school so often involves significant life changes that it is seldom undertaken unless there is a particular goal, usually a career goal. Sometimes, however, the goal that is chosen, and for which a major life change is made, is not an appropriate one. Of course, this kind of inappropriate choice is also made by traditional-age students, but the consequences of finding out that the choice won't work are not as difficult for them. If an eighteen-year-old comes into college wanting to be a historian and finds out that he or she really doesn't like history after all, it isn't too difficult to regroup and look for something else. If a forty-five-year-old man comes back to school because he de-, cided that twenty-two years of being a salesman was enough and that he wanted to return to school to become a math teacher, the realization that being a math teacher will not really work will be rather difficult.

Parental Influence

For traditional-age students, parental influence is often a significant issue. Parental expectations, either overt or covert, can cause significant problems. Students who come from high-achieving families often feel strongly obligated to enter a profession with the same kind of status as that of their parents. Sometimes, an assumption has been made at an early age that a son or daughter will become a doctor, lawyer, or whatever; and there has never been any question in the student's mind. In general, it is difficult for students to sort out their own needs and desires from those of their parents, and it is doubly difficult if the parents are attempting to live out unfulfilled fantasies through their children.

On the other hand, it is not uncommon for sons or daughters to aspire to the same career as one of their parents and for that choice to work out fine. In these cases the counselor must ascertain the degree of acceptance by the student and also his or her suitability. The conflict in these cases often comes when both parents and student agree on the career, but the student isn't able to produce the necessary grades in a required subject. A student who comes from three generations of doctors, and who has wanted to be a doctor for ten years, is in for a difficult time if he or she fails organic chemistry. It is a touchy and thankless job to be the counselor or faculty member who helps these students realize that their lifelong fantasies and those of their parents will not be fulfilled.

Sometimes in counseling, when you are dealing with the issue of parental influence on career choice, other more general issues relative to student-parent relationships emerge. The counselor may find herself in the position of encouraging the student to confront parents and behave more independently. This may be necessary, but it is also risky, because it can involve considerably more than just the career issue. As a counselor you need to be ready to help the student deal with the broader issues, or be able to refer him or her to a professional counselor to handle intense anxiety and conflict related to the general developmental task of becoming more independent.

College Major and Career Choice

Although the connection between college major and career seems obvious (one majors in something that prepares one for a chosen career), the relationship between major and career is troublesome for many students. For one thing, the connecting link isn't always very clear, particularly in the social sciences and humanities. If a student studies political science, how does that relate to a career as a political scientist? At the bachelor's level there really is not a job called "political scientist." A student might work for the government or go to law school or teach social science, but the career is not a *direct* application of the major. This relationship often needs to be discussed extensively with students when they are choosing a major. Many students have a tendency to choose a major in something that they like, and in which they have done well, without thinking through the career implications. The best strategy before choosing a major is for the student to complete some kind of career counseling or self-directed career exploration. He or she may not actually come up with a specific career, but at least the student will learn what opportunities are available with that particular major. The next section of this chapter will include an outline for a comprehensive career development process.

I cannot leave the topic of choosing a major without commenting upon the frequency of major changes among college students. It is not unusual for a student to change his or her major several times. This can be a good thing if the student is involved in some rational assessment of the fields and not just responding to a particular course or the need to find some courses for the next year. On most campuses there is a flurry of activity in counseling and advisement offices the week before students must choose courses for the next term. This is *not* the time for students to begin the process of finding a major and career direction. Career development takes time and, as you will see, requires considerable effort on the student's part.

Male/Female and Cultural Issues

The process of career choice is influenced by many factors in a student's life. The student's sense of self and attitudes as a result of sex and cultural roles can be particularly important. As a counselor you need to be aware of these influences and how they affect students. Although many gains have been made in expanding both men and women's horizons beyond sex-role-stereotyped careers, it is still not uncommon for female and male students to be influenced by these stereotypes. For example, some women continue to consider nursing as a career when they really ought also to think about being a physician. The counselor in this kind of situation should not force his or her values on the student; however, he or she needs to be aware of sex-role influences and bring them out into the open. A question to a bright young woman who is interested in the field of medicine, but who is not considering medical school, inquiring as to why she hasn't considered being a physician, is very appropriate. A similar question to a young man who loves teaching and working with young children, but who isn't considering elementary education, is also in order. These questions can lead to productive discussion and an opportunity for the student to reexamine attitudes. Similarly, in counseling a young African-American student who is strong in math, but who declares that he doesn't think he can make it in engineering, the counselor should raise questions about that student's assumptions. In a sense, these kinds of gentle challenging questions are useful for any student, but they are particularly important for students whose vision is narrowed by sex-role or cultural limits.

The opposite problem also comes up, often with women and minority students. These students may be keenly aware of society's previous (and sometimes current) restrictions on them, and can be very determined to enter a field that has not been traditional for that group. The counselor faces a real dilemma in these cases when he or she believes that the student's ability will not allow success in that particular field. With these students, or with any students, counselors should be extremely circumspect about telling them that they can't handle a certain curriculum or that they don't have the ability to succeed. We know from many research studies that expectation is a key ingredient in academic success, and we also know that motivation and persistence play a significant role in determining success. I believe the best strategy in these situations is to help students realistically assess their abilities and chance for success; and, if they are still determined, to encourage them to give their ambition a try. Of course, if they have failed a crucial course two or three times, it will be important to help them figure out when it makes sense to give up and try something else. Remember to keep in mind that giving up long-held career and professional aspirations is a traumatic and difficult task for anyone.

Setting up Alternatives versus Choosing

Before presenting a model for career development, let me make another plea for recognizing individual patterns of career readiness and choice. One strategy to follow when a student is just not ready to make a choice, but feels pressure to identify a career goal or major, is to help the student create several alternatives. The counselor and student can pick two or three possible choices and develop a set of activities and courses that will help keep the student's options open for a while. In the meantime the student can learn more about each possibility with the ultimate goal of making a choice later on. The following example illustrates this strategy:

Janet is an eighteen-year-old second-semester freshman. She asked her English Composition professor for help in thinking through some career issues and he agreed to help her. She reported to him that she has very strong interests in English, loves to write, and has seriously considered teaching, journalism, and law school. The law school idea is a more recent one. She likes the idea of being a lawyer and wonders if she would like legal writing and research. She feels that she should make some career choices and doesn't like the feeling of being undeclared and not really having a concrete goal to work toward. She did well her first term, but feels that the lack of a goal is affecting her motivation level. She is also under some pressure to pick her courses for next year within the next week. Her English professor wisely notes that she is not ready yet to make a choice and recommends to her that she set up her schedule to allow her the flexibility of moving into any of her three choice areas. He also suggests that she set a tentative deadline for herself to make some choices and that she devote time during the next semester to gathering information about the different options. In addition he also advises that she spend time thinking about her own interests, abilities, and values and how they fit into her choices.

This is perhaps too easy an example, since Janet was only a freshman and had some time before she really had to make any definite choices. Using the method of retaining several alternatives is more difficult later on, but is still possible. For example, if Janet were a senior, majoring in English, and still uncertain, as her counselor you might have to help her set up alternatives for after graduation. She might be advised to seek out employment as a journalist for one year to try out this profession (she could, of course, do this while in college at a student paper if she has time) and then evaluate whether or not she wants to teach or go to law school. Either of those alternatives then would require a return to school. If she sticks with journalism she may also want to return to school, perhaps part-time, to take journalism courses.

The key here is to help the student think through a plan and some viable alternatives. It is often necessary to help the students see past the boundaries that they have imposed on career choice. One boundary is often a belief that the choice has to be settled by sophomore year and that changes after that are not possible. Certainly there are costs to delaying career choices, but the costs may be necessary for a particular person.

High-Risk Career Goals

A number of careers goals might be classified as high risk. Wanting to be a writer, an actor, a movie star, a musician, and an artist are among these. In all of these careers only a small percentage of those entering the field ever make a substantial living at their career. In these cases it is difficult to help a student of any age temper ambition and desire with realism. Usually, as a counselor, you can't really provide any judgment on what the person's chances of success are going to be. You may be able to help the student evaluate the extent of his or her talent and potential, but in reality a certain percentage of the variance that determines success will probably be luck.

As a first step in working with students with these kinds of ambitions, I usually try to determine the extent of their motivation, dedication, and love of the area; and just how willing they are to take the risk of trying for what they really want. Their support system, age, and life circumstances make a great difference. If they are married, with children, then their ability to take risks is, of course, lessened. On the other hand if they are single and have some financial support from their family, then doing something like moving to New York to pursue an acting career may make sense.

One important key to this kind of career is experience. Anyone who wants to be an actor, writer, musician, or artist should be heavily involved in that activity as an undergraduate. The experience of acting in local theater, giving concerts, submitting short stories for publication, or exhibiting artworks all provide an experience of what it might be like to perform this activity as a career. The chance of success is greatly increased by a successful mentor. If the student has a successful actor, writer, artist, or musician behind him or her who feels strongly that the student can be successful, I am more apt to believe that the risk is reasonable.

The obvious way to deal with the risk of not making it as a performer or author is to consider alternatives to fall back on. Perhaps getting a teaching certificate is appropriate, or involvement in some managerial or business aspect of the field. Also, a discussion about how art, music, or writing might be seen as an important avocational interest can be helpful. A student whose greatest love is painting, but who also wants to go to law school, may be able to commit his or her career goals to law, but maintain a very strong commitment to painting as an avocational interest.

Graduate and Professional School

Questions about graduate and professional school come up in many career-development discussions. A large number of careers require several years of advanced study and training. A number of factors need to be considered: financial resources, grades and admissibility, commitment, certainty of choice, relationships, and other life circumstances. In a sense, choosing a career that involves further training also involves considerable risk. If a student chooses to go to graduate or professional school, he or she is risking the time, energy, and money required against the possibility that he or she will be successful and find the career rewarding.

Sometimes postponing decisions about graduate and professional school is the best strategy. One obvious way to do this is for students to work for a few years after obtaining their undergraduate degree before deciding about graduate school. Here again, readiness is important. Students must determine their degree of commitment and willingness to pursue a particular field. In counseling students early in their undergraduate career about graduate and professional school, the "keep your alternatives open" strategy is well advised. That is, a student can decide to apply for graduate school and also look for employment at the same time. Much of the readiness to choose depends upon how strongly the student feels about the career and how much he or she knows about it. If students have been able to work or volunteer in a medical, legal, or other career area, they will have a much better idea of what it might be like for them. In general it is a good idea for a student to gain some real-life experience prior to committing to any career area.

Model for Career Choice

The process of choosing a career is often not given enough time and energy by students and college faculty, staff, and advisors. Choosing a major is only a part of what should be a rational and considered process of thinking about one's future career and life-style. In working with students who have career-choice questions, I highly recommend the processes outlined here. If you can take students through the recommended steps, their chances of making a good (for them) career choice will be greatly enhanced.

The model of career development recommended here, which is fairly common in one variation or other, involves a six-step process. These steps include: (1) self-assessment,

(2) generating alternatives, (3) gathering career information, (4) gaining experience, (5) decision making, and (6) planning and implementation.

(1) Self-Assessment

This is the most difficult and probably the most time-consuming step. For traditional-age college students the task of defining themselves and their values is part of the ongoing process of maturation and identity formation. They may not yet have a very clear picture of themselves and they may not be very clear about what they want out of life. For older adult returning students, the decision to return or go to college for the first time is probably a result of a major self-assessment related to their decision to attend college. The impact of their self-assessment is great on their lives, and career counseling can be very important to them if their initial self-assessment was not accurate or if it led to a career choice that isn't working for them. It should be obvious, in either of these cases, that career counseling can, and usually does, have a strong emotional component. Helping a student find a career is not just a rational process of determining the right peg for the right hole.

A number of activities will be suggested to facilitate self-assessment. Some of these involve psychological tests and career-guidance computer systems. A nonprofessional counselor (faculty member, staff member, advisor, or other person working with college students) has some choices in terms of how he or she can be involved in career counseling. One choice would be to take on the major counselor role and set up several sessions with a student to help guide him or her through the process. If you take this route and you want to use various tests or computer guidance systems, you will have to work cooperatively with the counseling or career development center on campus to make these tools available to the student. Another role that you might take would be one as a kind of secondary career counselor referring the student to the campus counseling or career-development center. In this case you might check in with the student periodically to see how his or her career search is going, and serve as a kind of mentor and motivator. Motivation, by the way, is one of the major difficulties in career counseling. Many students do not want to take the time or energy to go through an extensive career development process. The counselor often serves in part as a motivator.

Remember, also, that you may deal with a student only at a particular time in the process. For example, you may be called upon for help in sorting out career information after the student has already gone through the early steps, or you may just have a few conversations that help a student learn more about his or her interests and values. Whatever role you take, the following suggestions for self-assessment should help you work with students:

Personal Discussion. Just talking about interests, values, personality, and life plans is important. The chance to talk with a successful adult who can help by asking good questions and by summarizing what he or she hears can be enormously helpful to a student. This certainly doesn't have to be done by a professional counselor, but it does need to be done by someone who has some good counseling and listening skills.

Course or Workshop. Many campuses have career development courses and workshops available to students. Working through a structured program with a number of other students has some decided advantage. Learning about how other students are dealing with career issues can help alleviate anxiety, provide good ideas, and build motivation. Often these courses and workshops provide a number of different activities that help facilitate growth in the different career-development stages. They also help teach students a model to use in their career and life development process.

Interest and Personality Inventories. These inventories can be very helpful in providing information for students to consider. They are not magical and they do not tell a student what to major in and pursue as a life career. Unfortunately, many students, and the public at large, place too much emphasis on these instruments. Part of the counselor's job is to help put the test information into perspective. Interest inventories generally compare a student's interests with those of people who are already in various careers. They usually use some kind of system that helps organize interests and careers into understandable categories. These inventories usually take less than an hour to complete and are typically computer scored with a profile that explains the results. They can be particularly useful in helping a student think about the careers that seem to match his or her interests. Students often confuse the results of these inventories and tend to think that the instrument is telling them what they would be good at. These inventories do not give information on ability, only interests.

Personality inventories provide a way for a student to look at his or her general way of dealing with the world and with others. I have described one personality system based on Jungian psychology in an earlier chapter. This system is based on a theory of preferences. Other inventories are available that are based on different theories, such as need structure or interpersonal functioning. Again, none of these inventories are magical, and they should be used only as a taking-off point to help students define and evaluate personality factors in career choice. Sometimes students need help in figuring out how personality relates to a career. Even if you don't use a personality inventory with students you should devote some time to a discussion of personality and careers.

Ability Tests/Assessment. The question of ability relative to career choice is always crucial. How can students predict whether they have the ability to go into a particular career? This is a very tricky issue because so many other factors like motivation, organization, and ambition are also crucial. Just having the ability doesn't mean that someone will be a successful engineer. Someone with marginal ability but great desire may do much better than someone with great ability and little ambition. The best gauge of ability is really past performance. If a student has done well in a particular discipline, then he or she is likely to continue to do well. Of course, the move from high school to college or even from one instructor to another can complicate this principle.

Most college students already have a test score that provides them with a general assessment of their verbal and quantitative ability—the SAT or the ACT. These scores and local norms are usually available to college faculty and advisors. The local norms are important. A student may be in the eightieth percentile when compared with all new college students, but only in the fortieth percentile at his or her particular institution. Counselors need to have a clear understanding of what these scores mean before interpreting them to students. I would suggest using them very judiciously, because they may not accurately represent a student's specific ability in a particular subject and they may not be fair measures of ability for minority students. They can be used as a general indicator and at least signal the counselor to attend to the question of ability if a student is attempting a curriculum with a score that is atypically low for that field (e.g., a student with a below-average math score is considering engineering).

Value Clarification. Career choice is not just a matching of a particular career to a student's interests and abilities. Although they are sometimes not considered explicitly, values are important in career choice. A student's values help determine the kind of vision that he or she has for the future. If serving humanity is a paramount value for a student, then he or she will seek a career and life-style that allows for this value to be achieved. If being wealthy and owning a BMW is a primary value, then a career that provides the necessary income is required. If scholarship and books are high on a student's value list, then a scholarly career, perhaps some kind of college teaching or research, may be in order.

Most students assume the value structure that is prominent in their family and in their particular peer group. In recent years the most prominent set of values for students and for American culture has been material well-being and achieving the "good" life. Many students in the last ten years have pursued careers in business, law, and other professions primarily to achieve a life-style of wealth and status. Although these values have always been a major driving force of capitalistic economies, they seem to have become more prominent in the 1980s; and the more humanitarian and social service values have become less popular.

Although I find this value shift lamentable, as a career counselor I must still allow students to make choices based on their own values. I would suggest that the primary role of the counselor is to help the student make his or her underlying values explicit during the career-choice process. Usually some value conflicts will come up and the student will become much more aware of the implications of his or her choice. For example, many students, when asked about the kind of life-style they want in the future, will respond that they want to be economically comfortable and have a good family life. They often already see the conflict between a good family life and strong commitment to particular careers. Many of them, of course, have observed their parents juggling career and family. A student who wants to be a doctor, for example, may need to confront the fact that most physicians spend long hours working—a student must give thought to this reality relative to his or her values.

It may be difficult for the counselor to deal with students whose values are rather antithetical to his or her own. I have difficulty sometimes with students who are highly materialistic and committed to making money as a major goal. My own values of service to others and family life make it difficult for me not to try to get the student to examine these values. In a sense this is inevitable; however, I do work hard at not being dogmatic, and at giving the student room to consider and then decide on his or her own values and life-style goals. I also believe that the career counselor should point out any conflicting values relative to career choice. For example, when a student chooses secondary-school teaching as a career, I believe it quite appropriate for the counselor to ask about how the student is going to deal with the income limitations of that career.

Personal Skill/Talent Assessment. In thinking about their personal and professional assets students often overlook the skills and talents that they have already developed. Skills like the ability to organize, which they may have developed as a leader in Boy Scouts, or a talent for meeting and interacting with new people, which came from working as a sales clerk, can be very important in career choice. We tend, especially in a college setting, to think that academic courses and formal preparation are the only significant career-preparation experiences. This is far from the truth. Students bring many talents and experiences with them when they come to college, and many students have some outstanding skills and talents upon which they ought to capitalize.

These skills and talents can be identified and discussed by using some kind of structure to help students think through their experiences and talents. Career workbooks and workshops often have these kinds of exercises in them. A counselor can ask a student to make a list of experiences, skills, and abilities by thinking back through various work and extracurricular activities. A student's particular talents, abilities, and skills are also often noticeable during counseling and can be identified by the counselor.

(2) Generating Alternatives

The generation of career alternatives actually begins during self-assessment. Students should be encouraged to write down any careers that come to their minds as they assess their talents, abilities, and interests. This has often already occurred as a student has become aware of his or her abilities and interests. For example, a student who has a high ability in mathematics has probably already considered engineering, computer science, or other fields where advanced math is important. Or, a student who sees him- or herself as having a particular talent for helping people has probably thought about becoming a counselor, psychologist, or psychiatrist. This is not always the case, however. A deliberate focus on generating new ideas should help the student clarify and develop new alternatives.

Interest inventories and computer guidance systems can be particularly useful in helping students generate new ideas and alternatives. For example, an instrument called the Strong-Campbell Interest Inventory compares the student's responses to those of people in a variety of different fields, and the profile tells the student which career groups his interest pattern most resembles. This instrument uses a system of dividing up careers into six different areas: Realistic (technical, outdoors), Investigative (scientific), Artistic (art, drama, music, writing), Social (teaching, social service), Enterprising (business, sales), and Conventional (structured, business oriented). The student, in addition to getting information on comparisons for specific careers, also gets information on the grouping of his interests. Career-guidance computer systems typically have an interactive inventory that helps a student assess interests and perceived abilities, and then provides career suggestions.

In the final part of this step the student must narrow down his or her alternatives to a list that he or she wants to explore actively. This choice is the first of several that involve narrowing down possibilities and alternatives. The size of the student's list will depend upon his or her breadth of interests and in some part upon the career-choice timetable. The listing needs to be made with the realization by the student that he or she will be gathering information and exploring the different careers. This will take time and energy and may involve work in a career library, computer searching, or interviewing people in a particular career. I would recommend that this final list contain no more than five careers. More careers can always be added if further work indicates that more exploration is necessary.

(3) Gathering Career Information

This part of the process is not easy for students. They need help with finding the information resources and with motivation. The best place to start is to help the student decide upon just what kind of information he or she needs to know. I always suggest that the student develop a list of questions to use when searching out information. Some of the more basic questions usually relate to the following:

> Salary/advancement possibilities.
> Training, schooling, preparation.
> Job market outlook.
> Work setting and tasks.
> Needed personal characteristics.
> Titles/locations.
> Work satisfaction/burnout.
> Geographic availability.

A student may be interested in many more kinds of information, but the above are basic. The job-market projection data may be very difficult to find. One good source of this for college students is the person in the college or academic department who keeps track of graduates in that program. Also, the placement office often has some valuable information in this area. Sorting out titles and locations (within companies and institutions) can also be difficult. Discussion with people in the field can help a student understand just where people in a certain career might work.

After a student has developed a list of questions, he or she must then locate information resources. I recommend three general sources: (1) career libraries, (2) computer guidance program information data banks, and (3) people already in careers.

Career Libraries. Most colleges and universities have career planning and placement offices that maintain career libraries. These libraries generally contain a number of books and compendiums that list and discuss various careers in different areas. These go from general to specific. For example, the DOT (Dictionary of Occupational Titles) lists all job titles. A more specialized book might discuss careers in psychology or careers in medicine. There are also many specific booklets and books put out by professional organizations describing a particular career or set of careers. These publications are usually helpful, but vary considerably in content and perspective. Many career libraries have librarians who will help a student locate information on a particular career. Sometimes the main college or university library will also have career-information materials. The biggest problem with career libraries and written materials is getting current information. Careers and career information change rapidly and many libraries are not as up to date as they might be.

Computer/Audio/Video Information Systems. There are a number of different systems using computer data banks and audio and video cassettes that can be very useful. These systems tend to be more up to date because they are usually leased from companies that update them yearly. With the computer guidance systems a student can ask a list of questions about the careers in the data bank and then print out the answers for future reference. Audio and video systems sometimes describe and show work tasks and include interviews with people in that field.

Interviews/Discussion with People in Various Careers. I always tell students to go out and interview people in careers in which they are interested. I am always surprised by the resistance to do this by many students, particularly if they don't have any family friends or relatives in a particular career. Certainly, friends and acquaintances are good sources, but there is no reason why a student cannot contact an office, or business and ask for a short interview to talk with someone about his career. There are some organized programs where alumni in various careers are identified, but, if a student will ask, most people are delighted to take twenty minutes or a half hour and talk about their work. Of course, students need to be cautioned that they are getting individual opinions, and they also need to be prepared to ask cogent questions. The college or university campus itself is also a good source of people in various careers.

It may be necessary for the counselor to help a student figure out how to go about this step of career information gathering. In fact, the counselor needs to be active as a guide and reinforcer in this whole exploration process. Sometimes helping the student set some goals and times for their accomplishment relative to career exploration can be helpful.

(4) Gaining Experience

After students learn as much as they can about a particular career, they are still at a great disadvantage because they have not actually experienced that career. Even though they have read, studied, and talked about being a doctor, how can they really know what it would be like to be a doctor? If at all possible a student should get some first-hand experience with the career or profession that is being considered. This is not easy, but it can be done. Certainly, a student can't work as a doctor, lawyer, or astrophysicist, but a student can find employment or do volunteer work that will put him or her in close contact with a particular working environment and with people in that environment. Many colleges have cooperative education programs whereby a student can work for six months in a career related to their major. This is an ideal way to test reality, but unfortunately these opportunities are limited. A student may have to volunteer to work in a related setting. For example, a student who wants to be a teacher can volunteer to be a teacher's aide or perhaps tutor children, or a student who aspires to do laboratory research in genetics might be able to become a lab assistant or even janitor in a genetics lab.

This aspect of the career-development process is perhaps the most difficult to arrange. For one thing, opportunities are limited and it takes a rather serious commitment to do volunteer work or to accept employment just to observe a career and a career environment. If a commitment to some extended experience is not possible, a visit or an opportunity to shadow a person in a particular career can be helpful.

(5) Decision Making

At some point in the process the student has to make a decision. Sometimes the process of making a decision is, in itself, a sticking point. No matter how much a student knows about him- or herself or how much information he or she has about different careers, the process will not be successful unless he or she can make a choice. Normally, choice is a logical part of the process, and a student is ready to choose and proceed with the last step of planning and implementation. A number of blocks to choice can occur, however. Sometimes, students are so unsure of themselves and so afraid of making a mistake that they just can't bring themselves to make a choice. A student who has grown up with parents who are very critical and who punished him for any mistakes will probably resist decision making because of the fear of a mistake. Or, a student who has always had all of his choices made for her by parents will be unprepared to make this important choice. Similarly, a student from a dysfunctional family who is struggling with severe self-concept and identity issues will probably be unable to focus on a career choice very effectively. These choice difficulties are really related to psychological problems that go beyond the career-choice process and should probably be dealt with as separate issues, perhaps with a professional counselor. As a counselor confronting this kind of decision-block your best strategy is probably to put aside the career counseling and try to get the student some help with the underlying problems blocking career decision making.

Other problems with decision making are usually related to competing alternatives or difficulty in giving up an earlier dream that has been ruled out because of lack of ability. For example, a student who really wanted to be an engineer, but who just couldn't pass the necessary math and physics courses, may have real trouble choosing something else, even though he or she may have developed other alternatives. Or a student who is very bright and who really likes the idea of being a chemist, a writer, or lawyer, may find it impossible to decide on one choice. As I mentioned before one way to deal with some choice difficulties is to set up alternatives that buy a student time. Final choice can often be postponed, with a tentative decision to pursue two different paths until a future time at which the choice has to be made. This point might be a student's senior year when he or she chooses a graduate or professional school or it might even be after two years of work experience.

Although most students tend to see their career choice as a lifelong commitment, it is important for a counselor to help them understand that the possibility of change still exists. Many people change careers throughout the life span, and certainly many college students change their minds about college majors and careers. The idea that later change is possible, although perhaps costly, can help eliminate the feeling that a decision will be cast in concrete and irrevocable if it turns out wrong.

(6) Planning and Implementation

Once a decision about career direction is made, there may be a tendency for student and counselor to breathe a sigh of relief and enjoy a sense of accomplishment. Certainly a great deal has been accomplished, but one additional step remains: planning and implementation. As the final step in career counseling student and counselor should devise a written plan that outlines how the student will proceed with the planning and implementation process. The plan should include information on the following: (1) achievement of necessary GPA, (2) gaining relevant experience, (3) cultivating references, and (4) placement (either in graduate/professional school or in a job).

Achievement of Necessary GPA. Although many students are keenly aware of the need for good grades, it is possible to get quite specific once a career direction is established. Grades play a prominent role in both job selection and selection for graduate school. Often, settling on a career goal will help a student focus his or her energies and do better in school, particularly if he or she has been floundering academically without a goal. Motivation, time management, study skills, and life-style have all been discussed in the previous chapter.

Although grades do play a significant role in job and graduate-school selection, other factors are also important. A student needs to keep GPA in perspective. The difficulty level of the career field must be considered. If a student who decided on a very demanding field such as electrical engineering, even though she knew that the math would be difficult for her, achieves a 2.7 average, this is an exceptional achievement for her.

Experience. The experience and skill that a student can bring to a résumé or graduate-school application can be quite important. As a counselor you should help students think very deliberately about how they will gain experience in their career field. If they have already done some of this as part of their career exploration, it is certainly a good idea for them to continue, and if they haven't yet gotten any experience they need to get moving. Sometimes faculty in the department that a student has chosen can help with this experiential component. They may know of summer jobs available, or of opportunities as research assistants or other volunteer opportunities. Some campuses also have volunteer and student employment offices that can provide assistance. Sometimes it is difficult for students to see the importance of this step, and it falls upon the counselor to help them understand how crucial some demonstration of serious interest and realistic understanding of the work environment can be.

References. It may seem a bit manipulative, but students need to think very consciously about who they can use as references. In many of our large universities it is not at all unusual for a student to go through all four years without really getting to know a faculty member. Some planning early on will help a student determine a way to demonstrate his or her talents to at least two faculty members. This can be done by participation in research groups, independent study, taking several courses from the same instructor, or becoming some kind of teaching or research assistant. Contacts may also come out of extra- or cocurricular activities, or participation in department activities or governance.

Placement. The final step for the undergraduate student is placement in a job or an appropriate graduate or professional school. This involves preparing appropriate applications, résumés, and participating in interviews. For job placement registration with the college or university placement service is a must. Also, taking advantage of instruction in résumé writing and interviewing is crucial. A student's presentation to potential employers may be as important as years of preparation and hard work preparing for a particular career. A faculty member or other person working as a career counselor can provide help with this preparation and can also encourage the student to take advantage of what other sources of help are available on the campus.

Applying to graduate and professional school involves a great deal of information gathering and sorting. It is crucial that students have advice from someone in the career field for which they are applying. Some schools have specialized offices such as preprofessional offices, and some departments designate certain faculty as advisors. Getting help in this area, as in most others, will require the student to be assertive and persistent. The usual advice for students is to include graduate and professional schools with a range of selectivity so that if they don't get into some of the tougher ones they will still have choices at some less-competitive ones.

Considerable emotion is tied up in this application process. Being rejected after a great deal of work, energy, and planning can be rather devastating. A counselor can once again perform the role of someone who listens sensitively and helps the student deal with painful emotions and feelings. After that, you can help the student regroup and develop a new plan for admission or for some other alternative.

This chapter has contained a great deal of advice on the career-development process. I have included a fairly comprehensive career-choice model and information on a number of topics regarding career choice that are often problematic for college students. The model presented is, of course, an ideal one. Students don't have to go through all of the steps outlined to make a successful choice, but many of the steps may be crucial to particular students. My most important admonition regarding career development is to urge counselor and student to give it the time and energy it deserves.

6

Relationship Issues

The need for social contact and intimacy with others is basic, and we all struggle with relationship issues and problems throughout our lives. College students are surely no exception. For traditional-age college students, relationship issues are usually part of their normal late-adolescent development, and involve learning how to form more intimate and reciprocal adult-type relationships. The college environment offers an entirely new arena for these relationships. Older adult students who attend college also cope with many relationship challenges. They must learn to relate to a new set of younger peers and at the same time maintain earlier social connections. They frequently deal with conflicts between old and new friends, old and new values, and time constraints.

Racial and cultural differences, sexual orientation differences, and physical limitations also need to be considered when examining college student relationship problems. Being different or in a minority group of some sort can limit a student's friendship circle and cause specific relationship problems. An African-American student who comes from a mostly black community may have trouble dealing with a majority white campus and contending with the subtle racism that occurs. Or an African-American student who comes from a middle-class background and has never really encountered black students from disadvantaged backgrounds may feel great difficulty in making friends with these students. Similarly a gay or lesbian student who is trying to be honest about his or her sexual orientation and learn to feel good about him- or herself, may be rejected by other students who are homophobic. A wheelchair-bound student may be rebuffed by potential friends afraid to accommodate to some of his or her special needs. The diversity in colleges and universities resulting from racial, ethnic, and a host of other differences is both a great opportunity and a great challenge. One of the greatest learning potentials for students in a college community is the opportunity to encounter and learn about people from many different backgrounds and cultures, and to test out attitudes and feelings toward others who are very different.

Although a great many different relationship problems arise for college students, three general problem areas seem to include most of these: problems related to loneliness and isolation, interpersonal conflicts with parents and friends, and difficulties with romantic and intimate relationships. A student's sense of self-esteem and self-worth is a significant factor for problems in each of these areas. Sometimes a student comes to college with a very tentative sense of self. This can be a result of growing up in a dysfunctional family, poor peer relationships in school, or just part of the tentativeness related to developing a firm sense of identity. Even returning adult students who have a well-developed sense of identity may have a period of tentativeness as they restructure their life and perhaps change some of their values in order to come back to school. Also, a student may come to school with a generally positive sense of self and have it suddenly challenged by problems with the college environment. For example, a student who comes from a small town where she had a number of friends since early childhood and was perfectly content with her social contacts may at a university find herself isolated and without the skills to make new friends.

Loneliness and Isolation

Being lonely and isolated on a college campus, with thousands of other students all around you, can be devastating and quite depressing. This loneliness is often amplified for students by the expectation that these should be the best years of their lives, and fantasies about the wonderful time that everyone else is having with friends and lovers. If I let my memory wander, I can remember literally hundreds of students who have shown up in my office with these feelings of loneliness and isolation. Although the problems on the surface had nothing to do with school, they invariably had very negative effects on the student's academic endeavors. A young man who came in recently comes to mind:

> Jeff was about six feet tall and quite good looking. He had dark hair, was muscular, and had a ready and engaging smile. He was quite uncomfortable as he came into my office and started out by saying that things just weren't going well in school. He was a new student and was attending school on an academic scholarship. It soon became clear that he was terribly lonely and just too anxious to be able to make friends. He reported that others often started conversations with him, but that he just got so scared, and felt so much pressure to be cool and engaging, that he couldn't sustain a conversation. For about a month he had been avoiding people and sometimes skipping classes. He felt terrible about his interpersonal incompetence and said that he felt much younger and more inexperienced than other students. He was thinking about dropping out of school.

After a bit of exploration I discovered that Jeff came from a family where his father was very critical of him. He remembered always worrying about doing things the right way to avoid his father's criticism. He also remembered choosing not to try a number of things in order to avoid criticism. He grew up having one very close male friend. The two of them had few other friends and spent much of their time together. They were both very bright and inquisitive, and spent much of their time and energy on secret projects and enterprises. Jeff didn't make many other friends, and he and his friend didn't date girls or go to parties. He knew at the time that he wasn't developing very well interpersonally, but he always had his friend and never felt comfortable talking to his parents about his concern. He remembered his relatives and friends of his parents always saying that, with his good looks, he would probably break a lot of hearts. His closest friend had chosen another college and joined a fraternity, and Jeff felt somewhat rejected since the friend seemed to be leaving him behind.

This is only one example of a problem related to isolation and loneliness. Many other variations exist. Some students are not shy or nonassertive, they are too assertive or perhaps have some offensive aspects to their personalities that put others off. Some are afraid of relationships because of sexual fears. Others are overly cautious and self-protective, and yet others are not good looking or attractive and find that many people ignore them.

As a faculty member or other person taking on the role of counselor how do you deal with these students who are often sad and unhappy? Can a few counseling sessions help, or is professional therapy needed? Of course, there is no easy answer to this question. You may be surprised by the power that you, as a person who is not a professional counselor or psychologist, can have with a few sessions of counseling. The commodities that you have to offer—understanding, empathy, good advice (after you truly understand the situation), and encouragement—are often in short supply in students' lives and their provision can make a profound difference. On the other hand, if there is some more difficult self-concept or other more serious emotional problem involved, more extensive therapy will be needed. Since most campus mental health systems are oversubscribed and since many students will never go that next step to a professional counselor, it is often advisable to try a few counseling sessions to see if progress can be made. Of course, if the problem is obviously intense and involves a serious disorder, referral is probably appropriate. If you take this kind of experimental approach, remember that you may get emotionally involved with the student and you will need to be able to be clear about your limits and the necessity of a referral. A later chapter will discuss more about the referral process and making decisions about how and when to refer.

If you do decide to counsel a lonely and isolated student, what are some useful strategies? First, as always, is the step in which you acknowledge that you understand the student's feelings and situation and that you recognize his or her feelings as legitimate. As an adult who has probably overcome periods in life when you felt loneliness and isolation, it may be difficult to identify with the intensity and hopelessness that is often expressed by students. You may be tempted to downplay the intensity of feeling by observing that the student is young and has great potential for relationships. This message of positive affirmation is important, but very difficult for a counselor to give effectively. It must not sound like a dismissal of the pain, and it must not come until trust between counselor and student has been established.

Often a combination of what is called cognitive and behavioral therapy can help students overcome loneliness and isolation by helping them form effective relationships. Cognitive therapy basically involves helping students change some of the irrational beliefs and thinking that they use regarding relationships. Note the word *use*. The implication here is that the student has the power to change those beliefs or faulty thinking. Although it is not possible to provide adequate instruction in cognitive therapy in a few pages, briefly let me attempt to outline two main cognitive approaches. One focuses on irrational beliefs and one on the process of irrational thinking. Irrational beliefs are assumptions that a student has come to believe, but which are faulty. Three main irrational beliefs that are often present in a college student population include the following: the belief that one must be perfect, that one must be liked by everyone, and that problems and difficulties are caused by external events. Many interpersonal and other psychological difficulties are caused by these three simple beliefs. Students often don't admit that they hold these beliefs, but some exploration and analysis can often help the student identify them and understand how they cause difficulties. Once the student identifies the belief and understands why it is harmful, the next step is for the counselor to work with him or her to try to combat the belief. Take the following example:

Jane is a sophomore, studying engineering. She is doing well in school, but is just not satisfied with her social life. She frequently feels lonely, rarely goes out on Saturday nights, and is starting to develop a negative attitude about her entire college experience. Jane was an only child and lived up to all of her parents' expectations as she was growing up. She was the perfect daughter and derived much of her satisfaction in life from pleasing her parents and herself by doing everything extremely well. She came to college believing that she should have a perfect social life, including a handsome boyfriend and lots of friends. In reality she has few friends and seldom goes out with boys. Her perfectionism seems to interfere with her forming relationships. She is always looking for the ideal or perfect friend, who never seems to materialize.

In this scenario you can see that the belief that she must be perfect, or close to it, is interfering with her forming relationships. She is probably rejecting relationships that have great potential because everything is not perfect about them. Perfectionism is a belief that she has grown up with; getting her to change it will not be easy. In this case she will have to learn to accept something less than perfection in her friends. She needs to move her perfectionism down to a reasonable kind of goal so that she can still strive for excellent relationships without being blocked by perfectionism. The counseling approach, then, is to help Jane recognize and confront her irrational belief that she has to do everything perfectly.

Distorted or illogical thinking can also cause relationship problems. Following are several of the most prominent of these:

1. Tunnel Vision—focusing on one or two events, rather than the whole picture, usually the events are negative.
2. Black-and-white Thinking—person sets up dichotomous thinking and sees only good or bad, success or failure, no in-betweens.
3. Overgeneralization—conclusion is reached without sufficient evidence, often as part of an emotional response.
4. Faulty Assumptions—conclusions drawn on faulty premises.

Tunnel vision may cause a student to focus on one or two rejections by others, and not realize that he or she has had many other successful interactions. Black-and-white thinking can cause a student to think of him- or herself as a loser, someone who just isn't destined to have friends. The reality is probably closer to a statement that this student may never be popular with everyone, but can still have many good friends. Overgeneralization can lead a student to conclude that he or she just cannot be successful with dating relationships because the last two people he asked out said no. Of course, a generalization can't logically be drawn from these two instances. And finally, a student may assume that because she is not beautiful (false premise), men will not be interested in her, when the truth is that a number of men really find her quite attractive.

A counselor's role in working with irrational beliefs and thinking is really one of teacher and trusted friend. It will not be easy for the student to change beliefs and thinking, and the counselor must provide patient and persistent challenge.

This is best done after a good counseling relationship is established, and in a nonauthoritarian and very caring manner. The counselor may not always see an immediate result in terms of changed beliefs. The degree to which irrational beliefs and thinking can be changed is related to the student's current life experience and to the strength of the beliefs and the utility of the beliefs for the student. In many cases the faulty beliefs and thinking systems have come to serve as defenses against painful feelings. For example, a female student who believes that all men are not to be trusted may be protecting herself against the repetition of some earlier painful experience.

A behavioral approach in counseling basically involves a focus on behavior change. The assumption is that improving or changing behavior will lead to better feelings and a stronger sense of self. One important technique for helping a student develop more positive interpersonal behaviors is called *role-playing*. Basically, this is a kind of rehearsal for difficult interpersonal situations. For example, if a student has trouble asking someone out on a date, the counselor can help him or her in this situation by taking the student through a role play. In this case the counselor would play the part of the person who is being asked out and would help the student learn to confront some of the different responses that he or she might get. These rehearsals, with discussion afterward, can help decrease anxiety and can help the student learn the interpersonal skills that he or she needs in that situation. Most students resist this technique, so it requires the counselor to be rather positive about it and to feel quite comfortable using the technique.

Group counseling and skill-building workshops can be particularly useful in helping students overcome interpersonal anxiety and learn new and more positive interpersonal behavior. In many ways other students can be better teachers in this area than counselors. They are more familiar with the territory and are often able to be very empathic and understanding. Most campus counseling centers offer groups and workshops. These are particularly helpful for interpersonal difficulties because they provide a kind of laboratory for students to explore new ideas, perceptions, and behaviors in an atmosphere that encourages trust and support. For older-than-average students it is important to find a group or workshop with other older students whose life experience is closer to their own.

One other approach to loneliness and isolation deserves mention. You might call it an existential approach. Many students, particularly traditional-age ones, don't yet understand that loneliness is sometimes just part of the human condition. This may be particularly difficult for students who are strong extroverts from families where they never really confronted spending time alone. It may be helpful to explore a student's expectations about friendship and contact with people. Learning to be alone and to enjoy it can be an important growth experience. Obviously a student experiencing great pain at feeling lonely and isolated would not benefit from a discussion of the existential joys of being alone and responsible, but for some students a gentle introduction of this line of thought can be productive.

Conflicts with Parents and Friends

Student interpersonal conflicts tend to be with parents or close friends, often roommates. The nature of these conflicts is quite different, although the interpersonal characteristics of a particular student may get played out in both kinds of conflicts. The counselor, in these situations, is in a difficult dilemma because he or she is only hearing the student's side of the conflict. Often the only thing the counselor has to work with is the student who is seeking help. Since most conflicts involve problematic behavior from both parties, it is difficult to work on the problem from only one side. One solution to this problem for the counselor is to have the other party also come in for a kind of mediation session. This is sometimes not possible or desirable so that generally the counselor must work with only one party.

Conflicts with parents are common for traditional-age students. These can revolve around many different issues, and almost always relate to the issue of independence versus control. Unfortunately, in many cases the issues are compounded by unhealthy parent-child relationships and by a history of poor family relationships. The counselor has several roles in working with students who have conflicts with parents. First, he or she plays the part of listener, and someone who understands and validates the student's feelings and complaints. Another role involves helping the student deal with the strong emotional issues related to the conflict between wanting to be independent and wanting to be dependent. The counselor is also called upon to help the student come up with strategies of how to best deal with parents and parental communication.

In helping students with these issues counselors often confront what psychologists call transference and countertransference. In simple terms, transference occurs when the student unconsciously begins to have feelings toward the counselor that he has or had toward his parents. For example, he may at times feel or behave toward the counselor in very dependent or rebellious ways. If, for example, a young man who has never really had a good relationship with his father is talking with a professor-counselor who is about his father's age, the student may come to feel very close to the counselor and in a sense attempt to find a father in the counselor. This isn't necessarily bad if the counselor understands the phenomenon and is able to provide a healthy male relationship for the student. A problem can come up because of the necessary time and commitment. Also, the counseling relationship, by definition, is one that terminates, so the student needs to understand that this close connection may not continue. The student can, however, learn some valuable things about relationships with adult males that he may have missed as a child.

Countertransference occurs when the counselor unconsciously has feelings for the client that come from feelings that he has about some other person, often a son or daughter. A counselor may feel very protective and motherly, for example, of a student who is in great emotional pain. These feelings are normal, but need to be identified and understood by the counselor. They can cause a counselor to lose his or her objectivity, and, therefore part of their effectiveness as a counselor.

One very common theme for parent-student conflict has to do with performance. Many students want very badly to achieve academically for their parents. Sometimes there is a very clear demand from parents (you must get a B average to stay in school) and sometimes the demand is less clear (we just want you to be happy, but we are very disappointed in your grades). Very often a student has developed a kind of internalized parent and the conflict is more internal than with a real parent. Often part of counseling about parental conflict involves helping the student sort out his or her own ambitions for achievement. Sometimes an unreasonable parental expectation is involved, most often related to a kind of "living-out-success-through-their-child" syndrome.

Parent conflicts are not all caused by unreasonable parents. Sometimes students want the best of both worlds. They want to be supported financially by their parents and yet they also want to be completely independent and at times pay little attention to mundane things like grades or class attendance. Counselors, watch out for countertransference in these cases! You want to help the student understand obligations and responsibilities, without taking on a parental role. It is difficult, but there is great potential for counselors to help students understand their own responsibilities and perhaps some of their parents' point of view.

There are times when you as counselor might want to talk with a student's parents. They may call you, the student may ask you to talk with them, or you may think it is a good idea. Make certain that any contacts are with the student's permission. Although the laws regarding confidentiality do not apply to people who are not professional counselors or psychologists, the ethics do. There are difficulties with talking to parents. The counselor can become a kind of middle man, and wind up hearing complaints from both parties. A counselor can also find considerable demands placed upon him or her from either or both parties regarding a particular point of view. I tend to stay away from phone contact with parents. If you really need to see them arrange an appointment and seriously consider a kind of mediation session with the student present.

In addition to parent conflicts a college counselor often sees students who have interpersonal conflicts with other students. These are often problems with roommates or others with whom the student associates closely. Often they arise because the student is not assertive and feels that he or she cannot confront the friend or roommate. At times these conflicts seem trivial and tiresome to a counselor, particularly when the student wants to present a blow-by-blow description of an argument or conflict. One of the keys to effective counseling with these students is to help the student recognize his or her feelings, including his or her sense of anger and hurt. This does not require a long discussion of the details of the situation. Although some of these conflicts may seem trivial, they certainly take on a sense of importance and sometimes of calamity to the student involved, and they can interfere with school and with other developmental progress.

Lack of assertiveness is probably the major problem in these kinds of relationship conflicts. Usually one party just doesn't confront the other, or if one does the confrontation is so aggressive that it is not productive. Usually, a good role for the counselor in these cases is to help prepare the student to discuss his or her difficulties with someone else and confront their differences honestly. This may involve a risk of losing the relationship, although this risk is usually far greater in the student's mind than reality would dictate. It is, however, possible that the particular relationship will not work out. Sometimes this possibility is hard for the student to contend with and he or she needs to explore what it would mean to give up the friend or roommate.

These conflict situations are not always caused by lack of assertiveness and effective communication. Sometimes one of the parties involved has some serious emotional or personality disorder that makes getting along with others very difficult. If you see a pattern of these conflicts in a student, it may be important to look more deeply at what is going on for the student, and a referral may be appropriate. Usually, by asking, you can discern if a pattern of situations like this has occurred in the past.

Another particularly troublesome aspect of these conflicts with peers comes with a student's defensiveness and inability to admit his or her part in the conflict. Sometimes the student wants to use the counselor as someone to confirm how awful the other person is and how impossible it would be for anyone to relate to that person. Very often a student just has difficulty seeing what his or her role in the conflict has been. Some gentle questioning and inquiry about the situation and the other person's perceptions can help a student begin to be less defensive and more open to examining his or her own role. This, of course, only can occur if a level of trust has been built up with the counselor.

Romantic and Intimate Relationships

For traditional-age college students, learning how to manage intimate relationships is a major developmental task. The late teens and early twenties are characterized by the need to develop intimate relationships. Intimacy here is used generally to mean romantic relationships, although some students also struggle with intimate, nonromantic relationships. Problems with intimate relationships take on great intensity for students in this age range. Often the relationship in which they are involved is their first really intimate one and the possibility of loss or failure is devastating. Frequently college student suicide attempts are triggered by the failure of a romantic relationship. It is not unusual for a student to feel as if his or her entire life is crashing down as a result of a problem with an intimate relationship. During these times, nothing else, including school, has any importance. For older students problems tend to arise as a result of difficulties with a spouse or as a result of trying to develop new kinds of intimate relationships in a very different environment. The intensity of these problems for older students can also be great. The decision to return to school often involves high risk for the student, and one of the greatest risks is working out a modified relationship with one's spouse.

College student problems with intimacy tend to cluster in a few areas: loss of a romantic relationship; conflict with a lover, boy/girlfriend, fiancé, or spouse; fear of commitment; and general inability to form intimate relationships. As someone who chooses to counsel college students with personal problems, you will be faced with many students, both male and female, who have just broken up with a partner. Dealing with the loss is usually difficult and time consuming. The student must deal with anger, hurt, and fear about the future. There may be periods of depression and feelings of self-doubt and personal blaming. The counselor's role should be one of providing an empathic and understanding ear. The counselor should help the student accept the negative feelings and accept the fact that life will not be the same, and that for a period of time feelings of depression, anger, and hopelessness may be present. The counselor should help the student plan for these feelings and for the impact on academics. In extreme cases it may be a good idea for the student to leave school or to reduce course work. Suggestions to meet new people and begin dating again should be made with discretion. At times, these suggestions can seem callous and inappropriate, although I have experienced many students crying and depressed about the loss of a relationship one week, only to be cheery and upbeat the next after they have met someone else. The time it takes the healing process to work varies tremendously from student to student.

At some point during the reaction period, the student often wants to discuss what he or she has learned from the relationship. In a way this is an attempt to come away with something positive and useful, and should be encouraged by the counselor. The student will often want to make some resolutions about how he or she will do it differently next time. This can be constructive.

Older students also deal with relationship loss, but in some different ways. Sometimes the decision to come to school and to make a major life change also involved a divorce and a kind of new independence. There are usually positive feelings and strengths connected to this new direction, but also a great deal of hurt and pain often still exists relative to leaving a marriage of long standing. For these students this pain is often exacerbated by difficulties in meeting new people and in developing a sense that they can find another rewarding intimate relationship. Sometimes, the student develops a kind of healthy independence, and admits that he or she may be alone for a while and will need to learn to develop and draw support from close friends and other support systems.

The counselor also gets involved with the conflict phase of intimate relationships. As you have probably already seen, many students will hang on to relationships and continue in a kind of off-and-on cycle far beyond what seems reasonable. I have often found myself in the situation of wondering why in the world a person puts up with all of the negatives in a relationship when the positives seem so elusive. Although many adults also have this problem, younger students who have no real history or understanding about the potential of new relationships, and who have strong fears that this relationship is their "last chance," often tend to cling to already terminal relationships. As a counselor if you get involved in discussing one of these on-and-off relationship problems, beware that it doesn't eat up a great deal of your time. Dealing with the ambivalence and inability to act can be frustrating and somewhat fruitless. One strategy is to help the student confront his or her decisions about the relationship and its possibilities. It can be helpful for the couple to seek counseling from a professional to help them analyze their relationship dynamics and to either work out their differences or come to a mutually agreed-upon ending.

The fear of commitment is often involved in ongoing relationship conflicts. In these cases one of the parties is ready for, and often pushing for, a stronger level of commitment than the other. If one partner succumbs to the pressure and makes a commitment for which he or she is not ready, the results are usually disastrous. Sometimes the need for commitment from one party is a result of a lack of self-confidence and the need to kind of lock in the other person so as not to be lost. Just as likely is the situation where one person is dragging his or her feet because he or she has not formed a strong enough personal identity to make a commitment to someone else. The timing factor involved here is hard for students to understand. Two people can be madly in love and very happy with each other, but the timing for commitment may just not work out. The counselor's role in this kind of problem is mainly to point out the timing factor and help students consider it and their own personal readiness for commitment. The counselor also has a role in helping students respect their own readiness level and avoid being pressured into something that doesn't fit for them.

Perhaps the saddest kind of intimacy problem is the person who wants an intimate relationship and can't seem to manage it. Often these people are just not competent interpersonally, so that they haven't really mastered the early relationship skills that help them meet other people. These situations were discussed earlier under loneliness and isolation. Other people have perfectly good basic interpersonal skills, but always seem to back off from intimacy. These situations are usually rather complicated and involve feelings and behaviors that are part of the student's personal dynamics. There may be fears of sexuality, identity problems, unconscious emotional problems, and many other causes. A referral is probably the best approach.

In summary, my best advice to a faculty member or other

person acting as counselor to a student with relationship problems is to be circumspect about what you can and cannot do. If you contract with a student to spend time with them on one of these problem areas, remember that these problems are not easily dealt with and can be quite frustrating to both student and counselor. The dynamics are complicated and strong feeling and emotion are almost always present. Behavioral and cognitive approaches that are somewhat superficial, but quite powerful are your best approaches for use with short-term counseling. If deeper counseling and analysis of past history and family dynamics are necessary a referral is clearly in order.

7

Sexuality

The problems and difficulties that college students have with sex and their own sexuality are similar in many ways to the problems that other adults have with sex in our society. Traditional-age college students do experience particular problems and issues as a result of their age and developmental level. A significant part of the need to form intimate relationships involves learning how to manage sexual relationships. This is not an easy task in a society that has repressed, and is at the same time exploitive toward sex.

Whatever guidance your own values provide about sexual behavior, you can be assured that there are many others who have very different and opposing views. In counseling students about any sexually related matters the nature of their values must be considered. Even if a student's values seem to be causing pain, you cannot, as a counselor, dismiss his or her beliefs as unhealthy or unreasonable. Part of your job, if you are discussing sexual matters, may be to present some alternate views and to discuss the impact of the student's own views, but this needs to be done with tolerance and respect for the full range of values related to sex.

College student problems with sex and sexuality can be put into several categories: sex and the development of intimacy, problem pregnancies, sex and communicable diseases, sex and violence, and sexual orientation. College students have problems in all of these areas. Many of these problems may not be presented directly to you as a faculty member or person who is not identified as a professional counselor; however, if you take on a counseling role with students about various issues, you will surely run into sexual concerns as a part of these other issues. Because personal attitudes and feelings about sex are not openly discussed in our society, problems directly related to sex are likely to be hidden, and it is not altogether impossible that you could be the first one to hear a student express fears about being gay or about being abnormal because of some sexual practice or other. In order to counsel students in this area you need to feel comfortable talking about sex. A student is usually very anxious about the topic to start with, so the counselor needs to be relaxed, comfortable, and matter-of-fact about whatever is discussed. If this isn't possible for you, it is perfectly acceptable to tell a student that you are not comfortable talking to them in this area and to recommend a professional counselor or psychologist. Many problems relating to sex will probably need to be referred. Much of what follows is for your information and background, and is not necessarily to be used in counseling sessions with students.

Sex and the Development of Intimacy

Students learn to express their sexuality at very different rates. Some students come to college with considerable sexual experience and others have never even dated and certainly have not had sexual experience. All students, however, have thought about and dealt with their sexual feelings. Almost all of them have an active fantasy life, masturbate regularly, and dream about ideal sexual partners. Men and women express their sexual feelings somewhat differently because of socialization and biological differences. Women typically see sex as part of an ongoing, loving relationship that is rather directly connected to other feelings of affection. Men also see sex this way, but they are also likely to experience sex as separate from relationships and as a pleasure and act in itself. Men and women are aroused in different ways and men sometimes feel an urgency earlier in the arousal cycle. For men, the development of an intimate relationship often helps them learn that sex and love go together.

These male and female differences, as well as the intense anxiety and incredible importance that students place on sex (learned at an early age from TV, movies, books, magazines, etc.), lead to many different developmental problems. Male students who are involved in an intimate relationship sometimes experience sexual dysfunctions like impotence and premature ejaculation. Females most often report problems with being nonorgasmic. Impotence occurs when a male cannot get, or keep an erection, and premature ejaculation describes a male who reaches climax so quickly that his partner really doesn't have time to become adequately aroused. When a woman is nonorgasmic she is unable to reach her own climax and sometimes doesn't find intercourse fulfilling. Although being impotent or ejaculating prematurely and being nonorgasmic can be caused by physical and psychological difficulties, for traditional-age college students they are most often related to lack of knowledge, anxiety, and relationship difficulties that negatively affect sexual behavior. I remember in particular one young couple who came in to see me reporting that their sex life was unsatisfactory:

> Marlene and Jack reported that they really didn't enjoy sex that much and that it always felt too hurried and mechanical. Jack reported that he was sometimes impotent and unable to perform, and that when he did perform he frequently ejaculated too quickly. Marlene said that she seldom reached orgasm and that, although she really loved Jack, she just couldn't seem to get emotionally involved in sex.

As I talked with this couple I learned that they both lived in the same dormitory and that the only time that they were alone and could have sex was when Marlene's roommates left for dinner early. This gave them about twenty minutes to perform and then get to dinner before the line closed. They were both attractive and well-adjusted students, who had been going together for about a year and who had deep feelings for each other. Neither had previous sexual experience. Both saw sex as a healthy and positive aspect to a relationship, and they were responsible in their use of birth control. They reported no previous sexual problems and appeared to have a rather normal sexual development. The problem, in this situation, turned out to be primarily situational. When they were able to have sex at a more relaxed pace and to feel less pressured and anxious, they had a very satisfying sexual relationship.

Another example of a more difficult case involves a young man named Bill:

Bill came in for counseling because he had been impotent the evening before for the third time. He was a virgin and really anxious to have sex. He was completely embarrassed by what happened. He cried as he discussed the situation and said that he felt like he would never be able to have sex with a woman. As I talked with Bill I learned that he was a very nervous and tentative young man. He had not had an easy childhood and had moved around a great deal. He never really had a relationship with his father and his contact with his mother was strained. He felt very badly because he arrived at college without any sexual experience and he spent considerable time worrying about his virginity and about his masculinity. He felt that all the other guys were way ahead of him and that he might never really be a man. His two earlier contacts with women were a result of bar pickups and he tried to have sex with both women in the back seat of his car. He reported that he was petrified of failure both times and that he drank a large amount of alcohol to relax.

Bill's problem with impotence was related to his overall sense of self and his anxiety about his own competence. It took several months of therapy to help him confront his fears and the problems he brought with him from his past. Eventually, he felt more confident and was able to have sex in the context of a relationship with a woman who was patient and had very positive feelings about him.

Many other sexual problems exist among college students. Difficulties with compulsive masturbation, pain during intercourse, exhibitionism, voyeurism, excessive guilt, violent fantasies, and many other fears and anxieties occur with varying degrees of frequency. Some of these are a result of ignorance, fear, anxiety, embarrassment, and value conflicts, while others are directly related to more serious psychological problems.

Sex and Communicable Diseases

The fear of AIDS has had a profound impact on society, yet some studies show that it has not significantly affected sexual behavior of heterosexual college students. Most students understand the dangers of AIDS, and to a lesser extent of other sexually transmitted diseases, but they tend to forget their fears or are too embarrassed to discuss them during sexual activity. Gay students are more likely to have modified their behavior as a result of knowledge about AIDS, but even this group still exhibits dangerous sexual behavior.

Any counselor has an obligation, when discussing sexual activity, and particularly high-risk activity (sexual contact where there is an exchange of bodily fluids—vaginal or anal intercourse, oral sex) with students, to take on an educational role and to discuss the dangers of sexual activity and methods of minimizing the risk (condoms). As a faculty member or other person counseling students, you are probably not likely to discuss sexual matters very often, but if you do deal with students who are engaging in dangerous practices you have an opportunity and an obligation to try to change the potentially destructive behavior. If the student needs information almost every campus has an AIDS education program with brochures, presentations, and other opportunities for counseling. With the increasing numbers of AIDS cases showing up on college campuses, you may in the not too distant future find yourself dealing with a student who has already received a positive HIV test. This, of course, means that this student has or will develop a terminal illness. He or she may need support with classes, with plans for the future, or just with trying to survive and cope. Most campuses have support groups for students who are HIV-positive and these students may also get special assistance from campus offices designed to serve disabled students. The student should also be connected to the local AIDS network support community. Your role with a student in this case will probably be one of being supportive. Personal counseling and primary support will probably come from others, although your relationship may be a crucial one to a particular student.

Problem Pregnancy

What do you do if a young woman comes in to your office and tells you that she just can't complete a paper, and when you ask her why, she sobs and tells you that she is pregnant and doesn't know what to do? Unwanted pregnancy is not an easy issue to deal with either in the abstract or in real life. Even the brightest of students neglect birth control and find themselves dealing with a pregnancy and considering an abortion. They often need help in making the decision and also in dealing with their feelings after the decision has been made.

This is another case where values—the student's and yours —play a major role. If the student comes from a background where abortion is seen as sinful and evil, then it will be rather difficult for that student to choose that option, even if it seems to be the best solution. If, as an adult, and perhaps a parent, you talk with a nineteen-year-old couple who is considering dropping out of school and going to work in order to have an unplanned child, you may have trouble with your own strong feelings that an abortion makes the most sense for this couple. In dealing with this decision-making situation, it is important, first of all, to try to involve both partners in the decision. Secondly, the reality of the situation needs to be assessed. Is the student really pregnant? Has testing been done, or is it just worry about being late for a period? After the facts are determined, then a decision-making strategy needs to be developed. Both the affective and the logical aspects need to be considered. Questions about the implications of any choice are important as well as discussion of feelings and values. It may be necessary for the couple to decide against an abortion, even if it makes the most sense logically, if they just can't deal with the emotions related to an abortion; or, contrarily, it may be important to make the decision based on logic if the facts seem to make the couple realize that a particular decision is the best one.

The counselor's role should be one of support and gentle facilitation of a discussion of all the options. Referrals are possible; however, the student may not get an unbiased type of counseling at certain pregnancy counseling agencies. Some of these agencies are really not committed to allowing the student a choice. Probably the best referral in this case is to a Planned Parenthood Office. These agencies typically employ professional counselors and can also help the student through an abortion if that is the decision that is made. If you, as the counselor, are morally opposed to abortion it may be difficult for you to allow the student couple to make their own choice in the matter. The most acceptable ethical way to handle this position is to inform the students that you have a particular point of view and to encourage them to seek advice also from others with different points of view.

Although most students who have abortions deal with the depression and guilt effectively, some require additional counseling. Most abortion clinics have postabortion counseling that follows a woman or couple for several months after the abortion. Sometimes, however, the reactions may come much later and be connected to something else. As a counselor you may not even know that a past abortion somehow plays a part in a current problem of depression or guilt. If you do uncover a previous abortion as an event that is still painful, it is important to talk about it and about the related feelings. The student may resist this discussion because of the pain involved and, of course, he or she should make the ultimate decision about discussing it, but the counselor should be clear about his or her willingness to spend the time and help with the painful feelings. As with so many different kinds of problems, the nonprofessional counselor must decide just how involved he or she is willing to become.

One other aspect of abortion counseling needs to be discussed—the role of males, both as partners and as counselors. Unfortunately, the male partner does not always provide the help and support that is important during the period of dealing with an unwanted pregnancy. Sometimes the individual is not the significant other and the woman involved does not wish to involve him. It is always important to help the woman who is trying to cope with the pregnancy to find a support system. If the male partner is not available or willing, then a close friend is a good choice. Usually, a traditional-age student does not wish to tell her parents, although there are times when the parents can be very supportive and helpful. As a counselor you may want to ask the student to bring in a primary support person to any counseling sessions so that their role as a strong support can be reinforced.

Sometimes a female student will prefer to talk with another female about a problem related to pregnancy. Male counselors should recognize this fact and be sensitive to a woman's hesitation in discussing these situations with him. The counselor can make a referral to a female who can talk to the student.

Sex and Violence

The statistics about sexual violence in our society are very disturbing. Researchers in one survey found that 22 percent of the students on college campuses have been directly involved in an incident of date violence. Another reported that one in three women have experienced some form of child sexual abuse, and another that 27.5 percent of college women have been a victim of rape since age fourteen. Although the educated mind tends to reject these figures as just too high, the reality exists; and it is likely that you, as a counselor of college students, will be talking with both men and women who have been involved in sexual violence. Early experiences of sexual abuse and even more current experiences of sexual violence are often hidden and repressed. Students seldom discuss them directly. What you will see as a counselor is likely to be the negative effects on a student's general psychological or academic functioning. For example, a young woman who has been a bright, committed student, who communicates well, may become withdrawn, depressed, and unable to perform academically. Although there are many possible explanations for this set of behaviors, a recent rape is certainly one distinct possibility. Early child sexual abuse can be part of many different psychological and self-concept problems. The feelings that have been buried for many years often surface during the college years when a student confronts his or her own sexuality, the need to form a strong sense of identity, and the need to form intimate and sexual relationships.

Although a faculty member or other nonprofessional counselor will probably not take on a counseling role for victims of sexual violence, he or she may well play a very important role in helping the student take the first step toward recovery. Although it may seem uncomfortable, it is important to ask a student about sexual violence when you have some sense that this may be involved in whatever issue is being discussed. Problems with physical and emotional abuse may also be involved in many of these situations. Although many of these experiences can be devastating, there is effective treatment and help available for students. Some campuses have specific programs or counselors for victims of sexual violence, and any experienced mental health workers on campus have dealt with many students who have these issues. In the case of a recent rape or assault, most campuses and communities have crisis services and programs where a counselor will provide important support and advice on negotiating the legal system. Also, many campus police departments have special officers and programs to deal with rape victims.

The term *date rape* has become widely used in the last few years. This term describes instances of rape and sexual violence that occur with known partners, often dates. Many women have previously blamed themselves for unwanted sexual attacks during dates because they were out with someone with whom they consented to spend time. Fortunately, this line of thinking is changing and victims are realizing their right to control sexual behavior in any circumstances. Much confusion exists in male-female communication about sex, and a number of campuses have educational programs directed toward males and females to help them more directly discuss sexual desires and wishes while on dates.

Sexual Orientation

For a college student there are few things in life more difficult to confront than the possibility that he or she might be gay or lesbian. Most students who are attracted to members of the same sex have kept this attraction a deep secret for many years. Often, they do not act on any of their sexual feelings until they are away at college and independent enough to be able to explore sexual relationships without fear of discovery by parents. The guilt, fear, and uncertainty related to coping with homosexuality or bisexuality can create very significant problems for students. They may go through periods of depression and be totally unable to perform in school, or they may do well in school but remain basically unhappy and tense about a secret that never really stops bothering them.

In order to counsel students who are struggling with these sexual orientation problems, you need some basic understanding of homosexuality. First, being attracted to someone of the same sex is not, in itself, a psychological problem. Both the American Psychiatric Association and the American Psychological Association recognize homosexuality as an alternate sexual orientation. The real problem with homosexuality involves our society's attitudes toward people who are gay or lesbian. Psychologists describe "ego dystonic" homosexuality as a psychological problem. This occurs when an individual finds that he or she has homosexual feelings, but being gay or lesbian is dystonic (in conflict with) his or her own self-concept. This, of course, occurs because of the strong sanctions people who are gay or lesbian must deal with in our society.

Two myths seem to pervade much of the thinking about homosexuality. People frequently believe that a person is either homosexual or heterosexual. Actually, there is a continuum of sexual feelings that goes from being exclusively heterosexual to being bisexual to being exclusively homosexual. Alfred Kinsey, a pioneer sex researcher, first discovered this concept of a continuum while studying the sex behavior of a large number of men and women. Most people seem to fall somewhere on the continuum between being exclusively heterosexual and being bisexual, while a significant percentage fall on the scale between bisexuality and homosexuality. It has been estimated that somewhere around 10 percent of the population is more homosexually oriented than heterosexual. The important point here is that a scale exists and that most people, even those who live heterosexual life-styles, have some level of attraction to members of the same sex. The other common myth is that homosexuality is a choice. A person does not choose what he or she finds attractive sexually; however, he or she can still choose how to act on those feelings. Thus, some people who are attracted to members of the same sex choose not to act on those feelings and to live more accepted and normal life-styles.

For college students, problems with sexual orientation are most often related to the process of accepting one's sexual orientation and deciding upon a life-style. Panic, anxiety, fear, and hopelessness are not unusual for students dealing with this problem. Sometimes a student overreacts to a sexual encounter with a roommate or other friend, and believes that he or she is gay or lesbian because of one sexual encounter. Facing the loss of a lifetime dream of a family and children, coupled with the abject fear of telling friends and relatives about being gay or lesbian, can lead a student into serious depression and thoughts of suicide. The pain of dealing with parents who just cannot accept the student's sexuality can lead to a sense of bitterness and abandonment.

Several counseling approaches can be helpful to a student who is struggling with sexual orientation issues. As is usually the case, a nonjudgmental person with whom to talk can be enormously useful. After years of harboring a secret that is painful and difficult to confront, having someone listen and respond empathically can help the student really begin to confront the issues. A counselor, at the early stage, needs to help the student confront the reality of his or her own sexual feelings. It is usually worthwhile for the counselor to help the student make some assessment about the extent of his or her homosexual feelings and desires. This assessment is important because it may influence decisions about life-style later on. If the student's sexual feelings have been primarily toward members of the same sex, then his or her orientation is probably somewhere between the homosexual and bisexual parts of the sexual orientation continuum that was previously described. The closer the orientation is to the exclusively homosexual end of the scale, the more difficult it will probably be for this student to lead a heterosexual life-style. The counselor should not, however, assume that the student is ready to "own" or accept this fact immediately. If the student seems to be about equally attracted to men or women, then he or she is probably at about the middle of the scale and can be described as bisexual. Students in this category can choose to act on either same-sex or opposite-sex attractions. If a student has some homosexual feelings, but has stronger or more basic heterosexual feelings, he or she is probably on the heterosexual side of the continuum, somewhere between bisexuality and heterosexuality. Students in this category are sometimes caught up in homosexual feelings for a particular person or classmate, and come to believe that they are exclusively homosexual. Students in this category may have had some significant homosexual experience in their past with no comparable heterosexual experience so that they are quite unsure of the heterosexual part of themselves. Assessment of sexual orientation is difficult and, if at all possible, should be done with a trained professional.

After the student begins to explore sexual orientation issues that have often heretofore been hidden, he or she is likely to begin to experiment sexually. For males, this may be a particularly dangerous period because sexual activity may increase dramatically after years of repression. Male students need to be apprised and reminded of the dangers of AIDS and the importance of protection. During this period a student may also find him- or herself getting involved in a gay or lesbian student group. This can be quite important because it provides a kind of acceptance for the homosexual part of self that the student has probably never really felt before. For some students the counselor's role may diminish during this period as the student works on "coming out of the closet." Other students will go through a rather long period of experimentation and assessment, sometimes taking years to work through guilt and denial.

One of the most difficult issues, and one that a counselor is likely to encounter often, is helping gay and lesbian students deal with parents. Parents very often do not deal very well with being told by a son or daughter that he or she is gay or lesbian. Students are sometimes shocked by the negative emotional responses that they get from parents. The risk of losing their parents, at least for a time period, is very great. In counseling students the counselor must help students prepare for this painful possibility. A student who is still very tentative about his or her own sexual identity should probably not risk telling parents about sexual orientation questions unless there is a clear signal that the parents will understand. Being honest about themselves will eventually be necessary, but it will probably be helpful for them to wait until they are strong enough to cope with parental rejection.

The process of dealing with a homosexual or bisexual orientation sometimes takes years. Often, but not always, this process begins in the traditional college years. A nonprofessional counselor can be helpful and supportive at various points along the way, but often students need to have regular counseling or be involved in some kind of support group. Some students seek professional help in an attempt to change their sexual orientation. Although a few therapists claim that they can make this change, most psychiatric and psychological opinion holds that sexual orientation is not changeable. Counseling usually involves helping the person cope with the myriad of problems that a gay or lesbian person in our culture encounters and in making personal decisions about life-style.

Limits and Liability

As a faculty member or other staff person, you are not likely to be faced with many of the above sexual problems. Because sex is still a rather taboo and hidden topic in our culture, students are probably not likely to bring up these issues unless they relate to some other issues or unless they come out because of the warm and empathic environment that you provide. You can probably be certain, however, that anxieties, fears, and worries about sexual matters are present in many of the students with whom you have contact. If you believe that sexual concerns are important in an issue that you are discussing, it may be helpful to ask the student indirectly if it is a sexual concern. This plays an important function in that it lets the student know that it is okay to discuss these things with you. Some standard questions that will often elicit considerable information follow:

Is this problem connected to your sexual relationship?

Does this have something to do with your own feelings about sex?

Are you feeling stress or anxiety about sexual feelings?

One strong warning is in order, however, regarding counseling students about sexuality. Discussions of sexual material should be done in a very professional context. A person acting as a counselor should not encourage discussion of sex because he or she finds it interesting or stimulating. It is normal for a counselor to have sexual feelings about students, but these feelings must be controlled and it is highly unethical for anyone acting in any counseling capacity to have any kind of social or sexual relationships with a student counselee. Professional counselors and psychologists undergo considerable training regarding their own feelings and reactions to clients and, in particular, on how to handle their own sexual feelings. They are also protected by the professional relationship and liability insurance if a client accuses them of sexual improprieties. Although I have suggested that you might want to ask a student about the sexual components of his or her problems, I also strongly advise you to limit these discussions and to make appropriate referrals if the problem is primarily sexual. There is no easy rule to provide here, but you must weigh your willingness to be helpful and your comfort with sexual matters against the fact that your questions about sex might be misunderstood and misinterpreted.

8

Stress

College life can be very stressful. Sometimes parents, faculty, and others tend to idealize their college experience and remember it as that idyllic time when they had few worries or responsibilities. It may seem like that in retrospect, but to students currently attending college, the process is often stressful and frustrating. Students are under stress in many ways. All students, traditional-age and older, experience competition for grades, the need to perform, worry about how well their college work will lead to future happiness and success, and all the stressors related to adapting to a new environment.

Many of the major stressors on college students have already been mentioned. For traditional-age students the college experience includes stressors related to their major developmental tasks. The major developmental tasks for this age group are the formation of identity and the establishment of an adult relationship with their parents; and the development of a capacity for intimate relationships. These tasks are stressful for all students, even those who come from intact and healthy families. They become much more difficult for students from dysfunctional families and for students who have had troubled childhoods. For older, nontraditional-age students, the stressors tend to be connected to their changing roles and conflicts with families. For a woman returning to school after raising children, the change in roles is enormous. For men returning to school after working or being in the service, college life offers very different challenges.

The terms *stress* and *stressor* are commonly used; however, some discussion of definitions is important here. *Stress* is a term that has come to mean any physical and/or emotional reaction that involves feeling anxious, nervous, tense, or unsettled. Stress almost always has both a physical and a psychological component. We know that stressful feelings translate into physiological responses like muscle tension, faster heart rate, faster breathing, and sweating. These physical reactions are caused by a complex biochemical process that the human species has developed through evolution. This reaction is called the *fight and flight* mechanism. This mechanism evolved as a way to help our early ancestors survive a rather hostile world. They needed to be able to defend themselves physically and to fight or flee life-threatening situations. Although we are not faced with the same physical challenges today, we still have the mechanism and it still operates whenever we are challenged.

As a culture we are learning that these physiological responses, over time, can have very negative effects. Cancer, heart disease, arthritis, and a number of other serious health problems have been related to excessively stressful life-styles. On an emotional level stress can interfere with a person's general psychological functioning. It can sour relationships, cause isolation and depression, and interfere with healthy psychological growth and development. Performance in most life arenas is greatly decreased by excess stress and poor performance in turn can cause lowered self-concept and negative feelings about self.

Before condemning stress outright, let me hasten to say that stress is only harmful when it is *excessive*. Actually, much of the stress that we experience is helpful and stimulating. The challenges of life tend to be stressful and an attempt to avoid stress completely would lead to a rather boring existence. The problem comes when we experience too much stress over time. College students and most other people tend to identify stress as a problem when it interferes with their performance in some way, but the accumulated result of chronic stress is really more dangerous.

You are most likely to hear about stress from students when it is interfering with their life in some way. This is usually related to academic performance or relationship problems. In many ways stress has become a kind of shorthand for any problem that makes one feel bad. Stress is often related to depression and frequently students who feel stress about a number of problems become depressed because they get discouraged. There are many very different ways that college students experience stress. Following are two examples:

John is a college freshman. He is forty-two years old. He has always wanted to be an engineer, but had to begin working after college to help support a newly acquired family—he married and had a child at eighteen. He has been quite successful as a salesman, but now that his daughter is finished with college he has decided to come back to college and become an engineer. He scored reasonably well on college entrance exams and seems to be quite capable of the work, but so far he has done poorly because he freezes up on exams. Although he had the courage to come back to school, he has been very worried about competing academically, and he remembers that even in high school he had trouble taking exams because he got so nervous. He talked with a faculty member several times and learned how to relax more on exams and began to do considerably better. He and the faculty member worked on his stress in two ways. They talked some about his uncertainties and the faculty member helped him become more realistic about his abilities and offered him considerable encouragement. He was also referred to a stress-management clinic on campus where he learned several relaxation techniques that he was able to use just prior to exams in order to physically relax.

Sarah is a senior in astrophysics. She is about a B plus student and has never had many problems in school. She works part-time for the office of financial aid and in recent weeks she has been late for work and seemed very tense. One of the financial aid officers talked with her about these problems and learned that she has been very upset because she just broke up with her boyfriend of several years. The experience of losing her boyfriend was unexpected and quite devastating. She can't seem to get her mind off the loss, and she is constantly wondering what went wrong. She is having trouble sleeping and has lost a few pounds because she is too nervous to eat. The financial aid officer arranged to have several sessions with Sarah to discuss her situation and to help her cope with the stress of ending a long-standing relationship. Much of their time was spent discussing her feelings about who caused the breakup and also about how she would ever feel strong enough to try another relationship. They also worked on finding ways for Sarah to fill some of the time and energy that she had put into the relationship.

These two cases offer illustrations of different ways of approaching student stress. In example 1 the professor was able to help John modify some of his irrational worry about his performance and to offer some very important encouragement and reinforcement. Probably even more importantly John was able to learn some relaxation techniques that he could use to counter the extreme tension that he felt before and during exams. In the second case Sarah was able to talk out some of her worries and put them in perspective. She was able to become more rational about her part in the breakup and also to feel less pressure about future relationships. She learned that there were many other interesting things that she could do with her time and that she really didn't need to have a boyfriend to be happy.

Although many student stress reactions are more involved than these and are part of a deeper and more serious emotional problem, many are not and can be handled with relatively simple counseling and stress-management techniques. The following guidelines can be used to help students deal with many stressful situations: (1) help the student understand the *interactional* nature of a stress reaction and to assess his or her own stress problems and general coping methods, (2) help the student develop a generally balanced life-style and effective personal organization so that he or she can be resilient to stress, (3) teach the student some specific relaxation techniques, (4) assist the student to gain perspective on his or her problems and to modify irrational thinking about the problems, and (5) when appropriate, help the student clarify his or her values and develop a sense of spirituality that will allow them to learn more about confronting the frustrations and paradoxes of modern life.

Self-Assessment and Understanding the Interactional Nature of Stress

Most students and people in general tend to see stress as caused by external factors that are often called stressors. Students will report that a particular test, professor, or situation are "stressing them out." Use of the term *stressor* seems to imply that stress is being caused by some other person, situation, or event. The first step in working with students regarding stress involves teaching them that stress is really an *interactional* process. An accurate self-assessment will allow them to see their role and responsibility in their own stress reactions. A simple, yet useful way to view stress interactions is to use three different reference points: the environment (what is happening externally), the mind (what the student is thinking about the stressor and his or her interpretation of it), and the body (emotional reactions and their physical components—fast breathing, muscle tension, etc.).

Frequently it is not the stressor itself, but the person's interpretation (often caused by excessive worry and negative thinking and fantasies about what might happen) that causes a negative stress reaction. For example, an honor student who is accustomed to getting A's receives a C on a paper in a history class. He immediately interprets this grade to mean that his grades are going downhill and that he will not get into a good law school, and, therefore, will not be able to live out his life goal to become a law professor. He experiences great stress over this grade and is unable to sleep or to concentrate. In this case his interpretation of the C grade is quite irrational and, in fact, he has gone on to develop a negative scenario in his mind that makes little sense. The stress that he feels is not really because of the C grade, but because of his rather unrealistic interpretation of that grade.

Another example is the case of a young man who is quite stressed and nervous because he is afraid that his girlfriend is getting ready to dump him. He reports that she doesn't seem to want to spend as much time with him and hasn't called him for several days. He hasn't been able to sleep and has been having stomach problems. He is so afraid of losing her that he is unwilling to check out his perceptions with her. In this case his underlying thoughts are centered around his belief that he can't get along without her. He believes that he was very lucky to attract her and that another woman like her will never come along. He has been fantasizing about himself as a lonely bachelor living in an apartment with no friends in a strange city. His belief that she is getting ready to dump him may or may not be true, so his interpretation of her disinterest may itself be inaccurate. Perhaps she is just busy or distracted for some reason. On a deeper level his beliefs about himself and his inability to attract any other women make him very vulnerable to stress whenever there is a possibility of losing his current girlfriend. Both of these examples illustrate the importance of interpretation in a stress reaction.

Some students trigger a stress reaction just by worrying, without any real external stressor. Students who are prone to be worriers can spend a great deal of time imagining possible negative consequences to many different life situations. This kind of negative thinking and worrying is very difficult to change; however, an understanding that the worrying itself is responsible for the stress can be a helpful first step. Sometimes the emotional and physiological reactions to stressors seem almost automatic and it is difficult to identify any interpretation of the events. A student may have developed a kind of automatic stress response to a particular situation. A true conditioned fear or stress response of this sort is called a phobia. Students may be phobic to test taking, talking in a group, open windows (fear of bees flying in), or any of a number of other situations. Sometimes, however, what seems like an automatic response is really just a pattern of negative thinking and interpretation that has been going on for years. There may be a phobic or conditioned aspect to it, but there is also probably some kind of negative expectation and interpretation.

Stress reactions to various situations are also affected by a student's general stress level and overall level of health. If a student is always feeling overwhelmed, eats poorly, and doesn't get enough sleep (a description of many students) then their general ability to cope with stressful events will be lower. A kind of feedback mechanism exists within us that often causes us to react to tension and stress by becoming even more stressed. We become conscious of our nervousness and that in itself makes us more uneasy.

These messages about the interactional nature of stress, and the individual's responsibility for his or her interpretation of events, and for his or her chosen life-style are not easy ones to teach many college students. For one thing they require the student to assume responsibility for his or her own stress. In many cases there is, in fact, certainly a real and legitimate stressful situation, so that it is hard for the student to see that even in those situations he or she still has a significant role in interpreting the situation. In counseling students who are under great pressure, it is certainly not a good idea to focus immediately on their interpretation of events and their responsibility. The counselor needs to first spend time letting them express their feelings and trying to understand just what is happening to them. The assessment and understanding of the interactional nature of stress must be discovered by the student as he or she is ready to accept it. Timing is all-important here. The counselor must be patient and gentle enough to encourage and stimulate understanding. As in most counseling, early and heavy-handed advice giving and interpretation by the counselor just doesn't work well.

Balanced Life-style

In the long run a generally stressful life-style is more harmful than acute stress reactions to various events and situations. If a student is constantly in a state of tension and nervousness, he or she will have difficulties keeping up with the demands of college and will also be less able to cope with stressful situations when they do come up. Many students are in a constant state of trying to catch up. They find themselves rushing and hurrying from one activity to another, always racing with the clock and never getting on top of things. Part of this problem, for many students, is not being well organized. The type of effective time-management systems previously described, with a clear understanding and prioritizing of goals, can help a great deal. Sometimes this rushing and never being able to relax is a personality/behavior style. This style, along with a kind of general aggressiveness and sense that one must always compete, has been described as Type A behavior. This Type A syndrome, or at least some parts of it, has been related to heart disease.

This kind of hurrying and the feeling of never being caught up is difficult to combat in students. There is often a kind of cultural reinforcement. Students delight in trading stories about how busy they are and about how they will never be able to get everything done. They frequently enjoy describing "all nighters" where they stay up the night before a paper or a test to finish at the last minute. Their general appreciation of a balanced life-style is not great. Meals, sleep, and exercise are often haphazard, at best. As someone who counsels college students you are faced with the difficult task of trying to persuade students, particularly those who are troubled by stress and anxiety, to live healthier life-styles. Sometimes, this is akin to trying to tell your own children to eat vegetables.

Some campuses have health education or wellness programs to teach students about the importance of a balanced life-style. They tend to espouse an approach that values the integration of physical, emotional, social, academic, and spiritual aspects of life. The emphasis on the unity of all of these dimensions can help a student learn the value of each dimension. The physical dimension is probably easiest for students to see, particularly the importance of exercise. This is usually valued because it improves one's appearance, rather than because it helps one manage stress and operate more efficiently. The best counseling approach is to help students decide how to modify their life-styles to include things like exercise and nutritious meals. A schedule and some encouragement can often help, even a physical education class can be a useful mechanism. The appeal of being more efficient and doing better in school can also be significant to a student. Actually, almost all students understand the importance of a balanced life-style, it is just the method of fitting it into their own life-style that is difficult.

Specific Relaxation Techniques

Specific relaxation techniques are extremely valuable tools in stress management. Most of the techniques like meditation, self-hypnosis, and deep muscle relaxation work in a similar fashion. They make it possible for an individual to spend a short period of time in a state of profound relaxation. In this state both the body and the mind are at rest and the outside world is screened out for a period of time. A kind of conditioned relaxation response is learned, so that whenever a person sits down to relax in this way, he or she is able to achieve very quickly this deep relaxation. The practice of one of these techniques on a regular basis provides a wonderfully calming and relaxing feeling that seems to have a lasting effect for many people. It is as if the person's energy level and ability to cope with the external world are replenished. Practitioners and researchers have reported many positive life affects from the regular practice of one of these techniques.

The scope of this chapter does not permit a very detailed explanation of these techniques or their practice. As a counselor you may be able to teach students one of the techniques if you yourself have had training or instruction. If this is not the case, you can help the student find a course or workshop and assist in reinforcing the practice of the technique. In reality these techniques are very easy to learn and come easily to most people. The difficulty comes not in the learning, but in the practice. In terms of the effort expended, these techniques are probably the most cost-efficient stress-management techniques available. Although they only focus on one aspect of the stress-interaction process (the body), the sense of relaxation that they provide helps a person worry less, interpret stressors in a more benign way, and also offers a kind of calmness and perspective that encourages one to decrease the external stressors in his or her life.

Gain Perspective and Modify Irrational Thinking

It is rather easy for a college student, caught up in a kind of subculture that sometimes focuses narrowly on a particular set of goals or priorities, to lose perspective and feel that a failure or problem is a catastrophe. Effective counseling allows students to move out of what is often a kind of isolated and very negative internal world and to gain perspective on their problems. The very act of discussing something with another person usually helps one gain perspective. In many cases the counselor just needs to be an empathic listener and help the students sort out their thoughts and feelings and bring them out into the open. The act of verbalizing them and putting them together will often help give students a sense of control. I have often had students say something like, "Now that I've talked about this, it really doesn't seem as bad as I thought."

There are times when the counselor needs to be more active in helping the student confront individual thoughts and reactions. I have mentioned previously the importance of helping a student evaluate his or her thinking about an issue and to understand his or her part in that process, in particular his or her ability to change negative thinking and interpret events more positively. There is a tricky shift here, for the counselor, from being empathic and responding to the student's feelings, to pointing out some of the negative thinking and the responsibility of the student to make positive changes. First, a positive rapport must be built, with the student feeling understood and his or her feelings validated.

Although I have emphasized the importance of thinking and interpretation, changing and improving behavior that contributes to stress is also important. Often the student can learn to challenge his or her negative interpretation of events and at the same time work on changing and improving behavior. The following example illustrates this:

Marlene is a first semester sophomore. She has always been a good student, but her grades have gone down considerably during the first semester of her sophomore year. One of her professors contacted the assistant dean of her college to discuss his concern about her precipitous decline in grades. He reported that Marlene looked upset and that she seem distracted and was often unable to concentrate in class. The assistant dean agreed to call Marlene in and talk with her. When the dean asked her about her decline in grades she began to cry and reported that she was having great problems sleeping and concentrating. Further discussion revealed that her father had left her mother about two months ago and Marlene was in a constant state of worry about her mother. Marlene was afraid that her mother could not go on alone and that she might commit suicide. She reported that she talked with her mother at least once a day and that her mother was always very depressed and just didn't know where to turn. Her mother did spend time talking with her own sister at home, but she couldn't seem to get over the fact that her husband of many years had left her. Marlene just couldn't stop worrying about her mother. It was as if she had put her own life on hold and even felt guilty because of her mother's problems. They had always been very close and in many ways Marlene and her mother were just beginning to deal with the fact that Marlene was growing up and becoming independent. The dean decided to talk with Marlene a few times and try to help her cope with the stress of constantly worrying about her mother and feeling responsible for doing something for her. After some discussion they agreed on several goals. First, Marlene would try to stop holding herself responsible for her mother's welfare, and she would try to counter her belief that her mother couldn't cope. This would involve combating the irrational thinking and beliefs that caused her to assume responsibility for her mother's welfare, and also would require her to take a more realistic view of her mother's ability to rebound from this very difficult situation. At the same time the dean and Marlene agreed that Marlene would cut down on her conversations with her mother and that she would try to help her mother establish other support systems at home. This would include some consultation with the aunt and probably professional counseling for the mother.

In this example the dean acting as Marlene's counselor wisely decided to help Marlene modify her interpretation of the stressful situation and also change some of her behavior. By not talking with her mother so often and by insuring a broader support system for her mother, she was able to feel less responsible and also to come to believe that she was less responsible. The counselor in a case like this also spent time working with students to help her combat the symptoms of stress, perhaps with some focus on more relaxation and calming activities like meditation or deep muscle relaxation. If Marlene's stress and anxiety symptoms had been extremely acute it might also have been appropriate for the dean to refer her to a psychiatrist or a physician for possible use of some minor tranquilizers. In extremely acute situations prescribed drugs can sometimes provide enough relief to give the individual strength to deal with the stressful situation.

Values and Spirituality

When stress and anxiety seem to be chronic and caused by students' general everyday interactions with the world, helping them deal with their stress and anxiety is more difficult. Often the student like this interprets many life events as stressful, and may have a kind of personality problem that generates chronic stress and anxiety. This kind of pervasive stress most often requires professional evaluation and therapy. There are so many different possible reasons for it. These reasons can range all the way from a history of sexual molestation to an undiagnosed learning disability that has created a severely negative self-image over the years. In many cases a professional psychologist or counselor can sort out the reasons and recommend treatment; however, in other cases the problem is not clearly definable and the best that can be ascertained is that the student seems to be blocked in his or her development or just does not have the kind of strong identity anchor that leads to good coping mechanisms.

In these cases, and with students in general, attention to the spiritual and value dimensions of life can be helpful. Sometimes a spiritual component or just a clarification and reordering of values can make a difference. The spiritual part of the student's life may or may not be related to a formal religion. If religion has been an important part of a student's life, and he or she begins to question basic beliefs, the struggles and uncertainties can create stress and anxiety. It can be helpful to refer a student to a campus chaplain to discuss these issues. Sometimes participation in campus religious groups will provide a forum for discussion of religious and value issues. A side benefit of these groups is often the warm and caring community that they offer. The counselor's role in religious discussion is limited. It is not appropriate for a person taking on the role of counselor to proselytize or push a student into a consideration of spirituality and religion, yet it is clearly appropriate for a counselor to recognize that dimension of life for students, and its potential for helping these students organize their lives and rely upon a sense of God or spirituality as a support with which to confront the world.

As I hope you can see, understanding and managing stress is not as easy as some of the glib articles about stress management seem to suggest. On the other hand there are simple and effective methods that can provide considerable help for students in managing their stress. Stress is such a popularized term and so widely discussed that it is often used to describe just about any ailment from which a student might be suffering. In many ways it has become a way for people to talk about emotional and psychological issues using language that is more socially acceptable and that carries less stigma. A major job for a faculty member, or anyone who is acting as counselor to a college student who is experiencing excessive stress, is to listen and help the student define and assess his or her own stress interactions.

9

Depression and Suicide

In over twenty years of counseling college students, my worst moments, by far, have been those few times when I have found myself talking with the parents of students who had committed suicide. Trying to help these parents understand why their children, in the prime of life, chose to end their lives is not something that I can recall without still feeling pain and sorrow. The circumstances in each of these cases were different, yet also similar. None of them had sought professional help (as is often the case), yet in retrospect they all gave out some signs of distress. The reasons for college student suicide are varied and complex. Sometimes students just tire and give up on dealing with a long-standing problem or feeling of failure. They may be unable to cope with an intense depression because of a lost love, or they may just not be able to cope with the pain of depression and hopelessness any longer.

Suicide is one of the leading causes of death for young people between eighteen and twenty-four, and there has been an increase in the number of completed suicides among people in this age group during the last several decades. Suicidal thoughts are not uncommon among college students. Thirty-two percent of the students questioned in one recent survey said that they had thought of committing suicide and 81 percent reported experiencing depression since attending college. In addition to clearly identifiable suicides, researchers have theorized that many automobile accidents and self-destructive behavior with drugs and alcohol represent suicidal behavior in college students.

Suicide and depression are difficult problems for professional psychologists and counselors to handle, and they are certainly problematic for nonprofessional counselors. Although nearly every student feels down and depressed at one time or another, assessment of student depression and its seriousness is difficult. The following information about depression and suicide should help you better understand student depression and its connection to suicidal thinking and behavior. As a general rule, a faculty member or other person acting as a counselor should consider referral for any student who is severely depressed or who has been depressed for more than a week or two, and for any student who exhibits any of the covert or overt signs of suicide.

Depression

Depression is considered a mood disorder by psychologists and psychiatrists. Because a person's mood tends to color his or her outlook on everything, being depressed has a significant impact on a student's entire life. It can be useful to view depression on a continuum with minor depression, often characterized as the blues or being in a bad mood on one end, and severe, life-threatening hopelessness on the other. In severe depression a person tends to withdraw from the world and may even have trouble getting up out of bed in the morning. Traditional-age college students often feel depressed when they cannot adequately cope with all of the stressors they encounter. Sometimes the combination of trying to perform and satisfy all of the demands on their time, and slow or limited progress in major developmental task areas (development of a solid sense of identity and successful love relationships), create frequent depressions.

Usually it is not very difficult to tell when a student is depressed. Most of us show our depression in facial expressions and body language. However, some students do manage to hide depression and give no clues as to how badly they feel. In addition to physical appearance there are many signs of depression:

Frequent crying, uncontrolled sadness.
Feeling apathetic, not caring about anything.
Inability to have fun or experience positive feelings.
Feeling personally worthless, generally unsuccessful.
Loss of positive feeling about friends.

Withdrawal from friends.
Guilt and self-blame.
Failure to take care of self, disheveled appearance.
Lack of energy.
Loss of appetite or overeating.
Physical complaints (headaches and other aches and pains).
Reduced coping skills.
Poor concentration.

In assessing the seriousness of depression the clearest indicators are length of the depression, degree to which it interferes with a student's functioning, and the intensity as experienced by the student. If a student reports being depressed for more than a week or two, this is probably a signal that he or she has not been able to utilize normal coping mechanisms to overcome a depression. Current life circumstances, and the severity and complexity of stressors or problems, are important in assessing depression. Usually short-term and minor depressions are related to a particular situation, do not significantly interfere with a student's life, and will begin to lift as the student gains perspective and begins to cope with the situation. Following is an example of one of these more typical situational depression periods:

> Mark, who was normally a very reliable graduate assistant and who took his responsibilities as a lab instructor very seriously, missed two lab sessions with his students in two weeks. His advisor noticed that he looked terrible, as if he hadn't slept well in several nights, and called him in for a talk. As the advisor began to inquire what was going on, Mark started to cry and reported that his best friend in high school, with whom he had kept in close touch, had been killed in an automobile accident two weeks ago. Mark said that he had been severely depressed since then, feeling that nothing really mattered. The advisor asked him about whether he had ever been this depressed before and Mark could only remember one or two other times in his life when he felt so badly. The advisor helped Mark understand his grief reaction and suggested to him that he would probably feel sad for a long time about the loss of his friend. He asked Mark to talk about the friend and to tell him about some of the things that they did together in high school. The advisor also suggested that Mark go home for a few days to be with his parents and to spend time with his friend's family. Mark took this advice and upon his return he saw his advisor again and reported

that he still felt sad, but that he felt able to go on with his life and his responsibilities.

This is an example of a fairly intense, but situational, depression. Although I suggested that depression might be viewed on a continuum, this example demonstrates that the intensity of the depression doesn't necessarily parallel the seriousness. In this case a situation created an intense depression that was an appropriate response to a real event. A less-intense depression that lasted for many weeks, in response to less well defined and more internal stressors, would be more serious. Mark was responding to his friend's death in an appropriate way, and he needed time to deal with his emotions about the death of his friend. His advisor wisely suggested that he seek some support from family and loved ones.

Harkum's situation is quite different:

> He had been coming into his honors seminar in American History looking depressed and somewhat disoriented for several weeks. He was apathetic and not involved in the class or with other students. He had also not completed the last three writing assignments. Upon being called in by his professor, he reported that he just couldn't get into the course. Further discussion revealed that he had few friends and that he didn't really have any particular goal or ambition for the future. He described his high school years as insignificant and said that few people liked him because he didn't talk about cars and athletics. He told the professor that he remembered being depressed on and off throughout much of his childhood.

This example of depression is quite different from the previous one. Harkum has been periodically depressed for many years, seems to be generally isolated, and may have a number of other psychological problems. In this case the professor would be wise to refer Harkum to a mental health or counseling center for evaluation and treatment.

Many other examples of student depression could be described here. Following are several very short descriptions with an indication of the potential seriousness:

> Jan is a sophomore who has been depressed for several weeks because she has a general feeling that she is not living up to her potential. She has not found a major and isn't really certain what she should study in school.

Although the causes of Jan's depression are not very well defined, this depression is probably not terribly serious and seems to be primarily a response to Jan's uncertainty about school. Some discussion about career and life goal choices, with career counseling and encouragement to take a more active approach to her situation, would probably help her depression. Of course, more information, particularly about her depression symptoms and previous history would be necessary before an accurate assessment of seriousness could be made.

Jeffrey has bounced between his mother and father since he was thirteen, and he feels immature, unwanted by his parents, and has a low self-concept. He has few friends and feels that he will never really make it in college. He has been unhappy for several years and his feeling of depression has gotten worse since he came to college.

Jeffrey is clearly a person who needs professional help. His depression is serious and is related to a number of personal psychological problems. It is not a reaction to a particular situation or set of events.

Marcia is a compulsive eater, is thirty pounds overweight, and is periodically depressed about her weight and her loneliness. She has a number of friends, but is not satisfied with her relationships with men. She is doing well in school and is in several leadership positions on campus.

Marcia's depressions are connected to some personal dissatisfactions and may be reactions to particular events that remind her of these disappointments. Her depression is not a simple reaction to a problematic event, and it does not appear to be caused by extremely serious psychological problems. Again, it is not possible to make a good assessment without considerably more information. Marcia's depression could become more serious if she begins to function less well and drifts into bulimia or some other more serious eating disorder. She probably needs to resolve her feelings about her weight, and learn to control her compulsive eating. Professional counseling or participation in a group or workshop could help.

Henry has been very depressed and upset for the last several days. His girlfriend of two years just broke up with him and he feels devastated. He hasn't been able to sleep or concentrate and reports that he has never felt so depressed. He seems to be obsessing a great deal about why she left him and he can't get past self-blame and recriminations about his behavior.

Henry is experiencing an intense reaction to a loss. His depression is probably situational and he is trying to make some sense out of what happened to him. Unless there are other complicating factors this is probably an example of an acute situational depression that will begin to lift soon. Henry probably doesn't need professional help and some counseling by an advisor, faculty member, or friend could help him sort out his feelings and stop blaming himself. Note the caveat in this example regarding other complicating factors. Intense reactions like this, although typical and usually short-lived, can also be dangerous and even lead to impulsive suicide. It would be very important to assess this situation and similar ones closely, and if there is any question, have a professional counselor assess or at least consult about the student.

Isolation and the loss of a love relationship are probably the most frequent causes of depression. Students who lose a fiancé or lover often feel that they can never have another relationship as meaningful, and in extreme cases even contemplate suicide because of this loss. Also, students who have yearned for companionship, and someone to love and to love them, may finally stop being hopeful that they will ever find someone. A simple failure to get a date for someone who has been trying for some time to establish a relationship can be the stressor that initiates a major depression.

For common depressions, those related to a specific situation or loss or the feeling of blues and being down in the dumps that we all get, there are some simple, yet effective, ways to help students help themselves. Although one common approach to depression is simply to wait for it to lift, a more active, coping oriented approach gives students a sense of control and a feeling that depression is something that they can handle in the future. Some researchers have suggested that depression is really "learned helplessness," and that people need to be taught how to confront and deal with depression actively. Following are some suggestions for helping students cope with common depression in an active and healthy way:

(1) *Increase activity level.* One of the most effective ways to combat depression is to do something productive or enjoyable. Students often feel apathetic and have low energy when they are depressed. Forcing themselves to go out, start a project, call a friend, or anything requiring action and attention will help the depression.

(2) *Work at regaining perspective.* Students who are depressed often start to see many different aspects of their lives in negative terms. Depression is often described as a kind of cloud hanging over the victim's head, affecting everything he or she does. Talking to a friend about depression and related feelings can help a student gain perspective. This doesn't mean that the friend can necessarily cheer him or her up, but a friend can help one to verbalize one's feelings and begin to gain a bit more control over them.

(3) *Take a vacation—get away.* This isn't always possible, but even a day or two away from whatever is stressing a student can be very helpful. Perhaps a weekend away from campus or a short trip, even an inexpensive camping trip, will provide the necessary distance and perspective. Often, depressed students need a bit of a push to do this. Be careful not to suggest a trip alone for people who need companionship or who might be more depressed than they are admitting.

(4) *Get back to regular exercise, decent meals, a reasonable schedule.* Usually students who are depressed have slipped out of a healthy and balanced life-style (if they had one originally). Just getting back into the routine of a regular schedule including, exercise, meals, and other scheduled activities can, in itself, be very therapeutic.

(5) *Set a time limit.* Many students experience depression as a result of a difficult situation or personal setback. Depression and sadness is really an appropriate response to what has happened. The problem often is not being able to move out of the depression and get on with one's life. It can be helpful to set a time limit for depression. For example, if a student loses an opportunity for a really excellent internship that he or she had been counting on, it is certainly appropriate to feel depressed. It is not, however, appropriate to remain depressed for weeks. Sometimes it can be helpful to allow one's self a certain period to feel bad, and even to bask in self pity a bit, if there is a clear

limit to this activity. A student may be able to gain some control with this limit-setting strategy. Another variation of this technique is to have a student set aside specific times of the day to feel depressed and to experience sad feelings.

Depression can also be related to biochemical factors. Considerable advances have been made in the use of antidepressant medication in the treatment of depression, although much controversy still exists over the best way to treat various kinds of depression. Certain kinds of depression seem to be at least partly biochemical in nature, and a history of frequent depression can indicate that a student might profit from drug treatment. A history of depression in the immediate family can also be a strong indicator of possible biochemical depression. The relative role of environment and brain chemistry is very difficult to sort out. If a person has been depressed because of chemical imbalances in the brain, the depression itself has probably had an effect on his development over time, and his learned reaction to being depressed for long periods may be as significant as the biochemical cause. Most colleges and universities have counseling and mental health centers where evaluation for biochemical depression can be done, usually for no charge to the student.

Another biochemical factor to consider in assessing depression is the abuse of alcohol or other drugs. Depression and mood are, of course, clearly affected by all of the most common drugs on campus. Alcohol, marijuana, cocaine, amphetamines, and other drugs are most often used to produce pleasure. Students who are depressed and unhappy are particularly prone to look for chemical happiness. All of these drugs can provide temporary relief, in one way or another, for vexing problems and ongoing depression. Unfortunately, their continued use and abuse exacerbates depression and can lead to drug dependence. Students are particularly prone to use drugs and alcohol to cope with depression when they have no other coping skills. The easy availability and lack of social control make drug and alcohol use common on college campuses, and it is quite likely that a depressed student will have tried his or her own "drug" therapy to deal with depression. A counselor is wise to ask about drug and alcohol use in any discussion of depression.

Depression and the propensity toward being depressed is

also related to a student's general personality and approach to life. Some students tend to see the negative side of life and to interpret events in a negative way. These students will experience depression frequently because they tend to see the dark side of most events. Often this approach to life is a rather ingrained personality characteristic and is not easily changed. These kinds of students can be very difficult to deal with in counseling because they often try to argue away any positive encouragement or interpretations offered by the counselor. Sometimes a cognitive approach (as was previously described) can be very helpful if the therapist is successful in helping the student change some of his or her major beliefs and ways of thinking. A number of studies have demonstrated excellent results when comparing cognitive approaches with drug treatment of depression. The key is probably connected to just how strong and how central the negative belief system and thinking mistakes are to the person's core identity. If his or her negative thinking is part of a defense system that he or she uses to cope with life generally, then it will probably be difficult to change.

Suicide

Students who are depressed sometimes think about and attempt suicide. As a faculty member or person who is involved in counseling you may uncover depression and suicidal thoughts when you are working with students. Frequently these thoughts and feelings are secret and when students find someone they trust and who is able to listen and respond to their feelings, they may share painful and hidden thoughts and feelings. Students may also allude to these feelings without mentioning them very explicitly. For example, they may express feelings of hopelessness or make statements like, "Well, it doesn't really matter," or "What's the use," or "I'm ready to give up." These feelings and statements don't necessarily mean that the student is suicidal, but they need to be explored. One good rule of thumb, whenever you have a feeling or intuition that a student has suicidal thoughts, is to ask directly. You can't always assume that they are telling you the truth, but in most cases a student will be honest if they trust you. Sometimes non-professional helpers are afraid to ask about suicidal thoughts because they think that the question will seem ridiculous or that they might actually suggest suicide by asking about it. Generally you are better off to ask and risk being wrong. It is highly unlikely that your question will raise the issue for a student.

Suicide and suicidal behavior are much misunderstood. Like sexuality and other topics that we would rather not discuss, a number of myths have developed.

MYTH—People who talk about suicide don't commit suicide.

FACT—Most people who kill themselves do give some kind of verbal warning. Certainly many students and others talk about suicide and do not kill themselves, but it is inappropriate to assume that because a person talks about suicide he or she wouldn't carry out a suicide.

MYTH—Suicide happens without warning.

FACT—People who commit suicide usually give clues and warning of their intentions. There are cases where a person gives no warnings, but these are the exception rather than the rule.

MYTH—Suicidal people really want to die.

FACT—Most suicidal people, particularly students, are terribly ambivalent about wanting to die. They usually vacillate back and forth, and only kill themselves in a period of extreme depression and hopelessness. Often people who unsuccessfully attempt suicide are very thankful soon after that they didn't succeed.

MYTH—When a severe depression begins to lift the risk of suicide is over.

FACT—Sometimes a partial lifting of depression actually gives the person enough energy to decide upon and carry out a suicide plan.

MYTH—Anyone who is suicidal must be mentally ill.

FACT—Most people who attempt suicide are not mentally ill. Suicide is usually the only way left that a particular individual can see to cope with his or her pain.

MYTH—Suicide runs in families and the propensity is inherited.

FACT—There is no direct evidence that the tendency toward suicide is inherited, although there is some evidence that biochemical depression is inherited and statistically the probability of someone committing suicide is greater if a parent or other family member has committed suicide.

MYTH—Most people are too strong to commit suicide.

FACT—Given the right circumstances and feelings of hopelessness, almost anyone is capable of thinking seriously about suicide.

Clearly, as a faculty member, friend, or advisor of a student you are not in a position to make professional judgments about the severity of suicidal risk. Psychologists and mental health counselors have extensive training in risk assessment and there are a number of psychological tests available to assess suicidal risk. Usually, if there is a substantial risk of suicide, a counselor or psychologist will intervene in some way and attempt to protect a student from harming him- or herself. The best strategy if you encounter students who are suicidal is to get them to see a professional. This may not always be easy and there may be times when you will have to decide what action to take if you feel the risk is great and the student refuses to see a professional counselor. In these cases you will need to use as much personal persuasive power as you can muster to persuade the student to seek help; and you may, in fact, physically need to take the student in to a counseling or mental health center.

Even though, as a friend, advisor, or faculty member, you are not professionally trained to assess suicidal risk, you will be forced to make decisions about how decisively to act when you become aware of a student who is, or might be, suicidal. First of all remember that you have no choice but to take suicidal talk, even in jest, seriously. Although you need to make every effort to get a professional evaluation, you may have to evaluate suicidal risk yourself. Following are some risk factors for which to be alert:

1. *Clear verbal statements of finality.* "I will be over this pain soon," "I won't have to worry about it much longer," etc.
2. *Isolation.* Any student who is isolated, lives alone, and/or has no friends, is at much greater risk.
3. *Suicide plan and means.* Any student who has a specific plan and who has the means at hand—i.e., has a gun and has thought about driving out into the country to shoot him- or herself, or has decided to do it late at night when her roommate is asleep

and plans to get drunk and then take a large amount of sleeping pills—is at very great risk.

4. *Chronic depression and hopelessness.* Students who have been depressed a great deal in their lives tend to be less hopeful about the future and it may be more difficult for them to recover from serious depression.

5. *Previous attempts.* Students who have previously attempted suicide are more likely to make attempts than those who have not had previous attempts.

6. *Giving away possessions.* This can be a sign that a student has reached a decision to commit suicide and is preparing to die.

7. *Sudden lifting of depression and feeling at rest.* Another possible sign that a suicide decision has been reached.

8. *Terminal illness or very limiting accident/illness.* Students who are dealing with the news that they have a terminal illness or who have been maimed or learned that they will be seriously crippled or physically limited may be suicidal, particularly when they are initially dealing with this information.

9. *Alcohol or substance abuse.* Abusers are at greater risk, particularly for "accidental suicide."

In many of the situations where serious depression or suicide may be involved, it can be very helpful for someone who is not professionally trained to *consult* with a professional. Most psychologists, counselors, and psychiatrists working on college campuses are very cooperative and are willing to talk with faculty, staff, or friends on the phone or in person to help them decide upon a course of action regarding a particularly troublesome student. In addition to helping you with the decision making necessary to handle a particular situation, it will help your own anxiety and fear a great deal to be able to share your concerns with someone else.

Suicide and depression are among the most difficult kinds of student problems for anyone to handle. Hopefully, this chapter has included information that will be useful in assessing depression and suicidal risk and in helping students manage common depressions. Although all of us who are part of campus communities do our best to get help for students who are depressed or suicidal, it is not always possible to prevent suicides. Although students usually signal their intent in some way, there are times when a suicide is virtually a complete surprise. It is important to realize that when a suicide occurs there are usually a number of people who are personally affected and who may need support and understanding. As a counselor of college students you may be one of them. It is natural to feel fear and anxiety about students who are depressed and suicidal. Don't shoulder responsibility for dealing with a student in this situation, seek out consultation and support from professionals and attend to your own feelings.

10

Alcohol/Substance Abuse, Dysfunctional Families, and Eating Disorders

A number of problems and disorders have become more prominent in the college student population during the last ten or fifteen years. Some of these have probably existed for decades and have only recently been identified and brought out into the open. For example, in the past, experiences with sexual and physical abuse were nearly always kept secret, and the pain and emotional abuse related to growing up in an alcoholic family were typically not discussed. Counselors and psychologists, until fairly recently, did not realize the extent of these experiences in the student population and they sometimes did not identify them in their student clients. Currently there is a much greater awareness, and counselors are developing new ways to identify, diagnose and treat problems related to these difficulties. The increasing awareness and willingness to discuss previously hidden experiences like sexual, physical, and emotional abuse are largely responsible for the dramatic increase in the incidence of problems related to these experiences; however, I do not rule out the possibility that there has also been an actual increase in the frequency of these experiences and related problems.

Alcohol and drug abuse problems, on the other hand, have always played a prominent role on college campuses in one form or another. The abuse of alcohol seems to be a time-honored college tradition, a kind of rite of passage in many ways. The prominence and use of other drugs seem to vary. We have gone through periods when LSD and marijuana were the drugs of choice, with cocaine, barbiturates, and amphetamines, all having periods of popularity. Although abuse of these drugs, and alcohol, has always had life-threatening consequences, the dangers seem to be increasing. The popularity of free-basing cocaine (smoking it in crystal form) and its availability have propelled cocaine use into a grave national problem. The average strength of a marijuana cigarette, which many once believed was relatively benign, has increased tenfold in the last twenty years, making its use considerably riskier.

The dangers of alcohol and drug abuse have also increased because of the AIDS virus. Studies show that many college students have unprotected sex while they are under the influence of alcohol or other drugs. Since the incidence of AIDS is still relatively small in the heterosexual community, the impact of this self-destructive behavior has not been great, but as the virus makes inroads into the heterosexual community of students, as it inevitably will, these dangers will increase. The use of intravenous needles by drug abusers has also become much more dangerous because of the AIDS epidemic.

The effects on students of growing up in families where one or both parents were alcoholic have been widely discussed in recent years. Some researchers have estimated that as many as one-third of our college students have grown up in these families. These students, called ACOAs (adult children of alcoholics), have been described in many recent publications. The families from which these students come have been described as "dysfunctional." This term has been expanded by some to include people who have come from families where any kind of major family problem existed that greatly impacted on their growth and development. This might include families where there was sexual, physical, or emotional abuse, as well as where there was alcohol abuse. The statistics demonstrating the incidence of these experiences are alarming. As someone who has worked as a college counselor for about twenty years, my own experience confirms the fact that there is an alarming increase in the number of students who are suffering the effects of growing up in seriously dysfunctional families. In my own musings I have considered many different aspects of modern life that might be responsible, but for this discussion the causes are really less important than trying to deal with how the college counselor or person working with college students can cope with the effects of a negative and hurtful family experience.

Another category of problems might be categorized as those that are related to society's attitudes and views about women. Many female college students suffer from difficulties with eating disorders. These can range from compulsive eating to problems with bulimia (binging and purging with vomiting or laxatives), and anorexia (a disorder where the individual starves herself until she is too thin). Bulimia is more often a disorder of traditional-age college women, but may also occur in men. Some researchers and clinicians have suggested that the disorders are more prevalent in men than we realize, but are more deeply hidden because of students' unwillingness to admit to what are essentially seen as female problems.

All of these disorders related to eating and weight control are complex and seem to be clearly related to problems in forming identity and developing a positive self-concept. Most clinicians and researchers suggest that they are directly related to society's unhealthy attitudes toward women. The desire to have a perfect body, to be the perfect woman as defined by the media and the prevailing attitudes of men, seem to play into these disorders. The obsession with thinness and the tying of a woman's self-worth to her physical beauty are clearly connected to our culture's attitudes toward women. Certainly other factors, such as family history and are also significant, but it is clear that the image of woman plays a significant role.

Many clinicians and researchers have also related problems with sexual violence to society's attitudes toward women and in particular the view by many men of women as sex objects, a kind of devaluing and dehumanizing of women in a sexual context. Numerous studies have shown that our media, advertising, and male socialization all contribute to the maintenance of this attitude. The prevalence of what is called "date rape" is an alarming, relatively new awareness for most members of the campus community. Various studies have shown that from one-fourth to one-third of college women will be victims of sexual violence during college.

The purpose of this chapter is to provide a brief discussion of the three major problem areas that have been identified as becoming more prominent in recent years. In each of these areas a student can experience any number of psychological and even physical difficulties. Alcohol and substance abuse, for example can spawn academic failure, low self-concept, disastrous interpersonal relationships, and many other serious emotional problems. Of course, there is some debate as to which comes first, the abuse or the emotional and interpersonal problems. Since these problem areas are so prevalent and so serious, information on symptoms, identification, and treatment will be included for each area. The goal here, however, is not to teach you how to counsel students with these problems. They are all too serious and too complex to be dealt with by a person who is not a professional therapist. They are, however, often not easy to identify and students are frequently defensive and deny problems in these areas.

Alcohol/Substance Abuse

Clearly the problems that college students have in this area are a reflection of the extremely difficult time that we as a society have with the use and abuse of all sorts of drugs. In many ways the college environment is ripe for abuse of substances. Traditional-age students are young and eager to have new experiences; they have a sense of invulnerability; they are under pressure and want to escape the stress; and they have just escaped the bonds of restraint and control provided by their parents. In addition, alcohol and drugs are easily available and in common use by many other students. Researchers have found, for example, that a higher percentage of traditional-age college students drink alcohol than any other age cohort in our society.

In this atmosphere where drugs and alcohol are often the norm, one must struggle with defining just what constitutes "abuse" of a substance. If a student reports to you that he or she was drunk last weekend and couldn't even remember what happened for several hours, is that abuse, or just a normal college binge? If a student says that he uses marijuana several evenings a week to help him relax and "chill out," does he have a problem? If a young woman plans to use LSD with friends on a free weekend to learn more about herself and her inner personality, should you be alarmed? And, if you do find any of these reports disturbing, what do you do with the student? In each of these situations you need more information to see if there is a pattern of drug abuse. If the student has any kind of personal or psychological problem, I would certainly look for the effects of substance abuse as a major factor.

There are actually several ways in which you might encounter student drug and alcohol problems. One way, similar to the situations described above, is the situation when a student openly talks about drug use. This would probably be in the context of some other situation and not directly related, at least in their minds, to substance use. Another way, which is not very common, is the case of a student directly asking for help with a drug or alcohol problem. In these cases the student has already experienced some very negative consequences and has decided that he or she needs help. Another way, perhaps the most likely way, that you will hear about drug or alcohol abuse, is indirectly. The student will be complaining about one of dozens of problems, such as poor performance, general unhappiness, stress, or depression that may be related to the substance abuse. As part of counseling students for almost any personal problem, their use of alcohol or drugs should be checked out.

There are a number of indications of substance abuse that you may see in students. The official diagnostic criteria from the diagnostic handbook that psychologists and psychiatrists use are divided into two categories, one for psychoactive substance *abuse* and one for psychoactive substance *dependence*. Following are the criteria as listed:

Abuse (All of the Following)

1. Duration of one month;
2. Continued psychoactive substance use despite knowledge of having persistent or recurrent social, academic, psychological or physical problem that is exacerbated by use of the substance;
3. Recurrent use in situations in which use is physically hazardous (e.g., driving while intoxicated).

Dependence (At Least Three of the Following)*

1. Chemical taken in larger amounts or longer period than the student intended;
2. Persistent desire or one or more unsuccessful efforts to cut down or control substance use;
3. Large amounts of time spent in getting the substance, taking the substance, or recovering from its effects;
4. Frequent intoxication or withdrawal symptoms, often when the student is expected to fulfill major obligations (e.g., complete papers, take exams, etc.), or when substance abuse is physically hazardous (e.g., driving when intoxicated);
5. Important social, occupational or recreational activities are given up or reduced because of substance use;
6. Continued substance use despite knowledge of having persistent social, psychological, physical, or academic problems;
7. Tolerance: need for markedly increased amounts of the substance in order to achieve intoxication or desired affect;
8. Withdrawal symptoms: hangovers, "shakes," hallucinations, etc.;
9. Substance taken to relieve or avoid withdrawal symptoms.

In most cases when students are dependent upon a substance they are at a point where it has physically begun to deteriorate them. These students look bad physically, they typically do not sleep regular hours, they are often underweight, disheveled, sometimes dirty, and they may even be incoherent or under the influence of something when you talk with them. Some of these students are in such bad shape that they may well be self-destructive. Some kind of intervention should be undertaken to see that they get help. This may be another case where a call to the dean is required to report that the student cannot really function alone any longer. There really aren't many students who reach this point on campus. You will have to deal mostly with students who are in the early stages of abuse and who are probably still functional and in various stages of denial.

Treatment of students with substance-abuse disorders can be classified as occurring in any of three stages. Stage 1 is counseling at an early point when the student is starting to abuse drugs or alcohol usually as a way of coping with some set of problems that he or she can't handle. It might be coping with loneliness

---

*Taken from T. M. Rivinus, *Alcoholism/Chemical Dependency and the College Student* (New York: Haworth Press, 1988), pp. 116–17.

and having nothing else to do, it might be dealing with a fear of failure and poor progress in school, it might be worry about dating and sexual relationships, or it might be lack of purpose. Most counseling of students at this stage is really directed at the problem or problems that students perceive as interfering with their life. Substance abuse is usually not seen as the major factor. Sometimes a bad drug experience or a blackout will bring a student in at this stage who begins to see the possibility of dangerous substance abuse consequences.

Stage 2 involves a structured and often mandatory treatment program that comes after substance abuse is clearly identified as the major problem. This treatment usually includes individual and group counseling that is designed to bring peer pressure on the person to stop using the abused substance. Most often in these treatment programs the assumption is made that the student cannot handle any use of drugs or alcohol. The group counseling might be participation in Alcoholics Anonymous or Narcotics Anonymous or some other regular support group. A major focus in this treatment stage is elimination of substance use. By the time the student gets to this stage he or she has demonstrated that he or she can no longer use the substance in moderation—this includes alcohol. Usually by this stage the dependence upon the substance is so strong that it basically controls the student's life. Many substance-abuse counselors, and particularly the Alcoholics Anonymous proponents, believe that alcoholism is a disease and that a person who abuses alcohol has a physical inability to handle that particular substance. After the goal of becoming substance-free is accomplished in this stage, work on learning to live life without the substance is begun. In many cases the student must work on this for an indefinite period of time.

Stage 3 treatment is the end of the line. It involves inpatient treatment in a facility designed for alcohol and substance abusers. This treatment is partly to eliminate the substances from the person's body and to manage and control withdrawal. Students who can no longer function typically wind up in this type of treatment. The nature of the treatment, of course, necessitates leaving school. Usually extensive outpatient treatment is necessary after the person is released, often with participation in a support group.

In dealing with substance-abusing students avoid "enabling" the person to continue the abuse. They should have to suffer the consequences of their behavior, and even though you are their friend or counselor, you shouldn't "rescue" them from the consequences of their behavior. For example, if a student doesn't have a paper done on time because he or she was out partying too much or fell asleep from being so tired as a result of a hangover, a faculty member shouldn't allow them an extension. Students often maintain their abuse because people around them take care of them and help them excuse their behavior and avoid the consequences of their actions. Most often a student will ultimately decide to get help only when he or she can see no other way to continue.

Advice and consultation can be invaluable in dealing with substance-abusing students. Therapists find these clients among the most difficult to work with, so you need to get as much help as you can get. Also, there are often times when students who are abusers refuse to be helped. No matter what you do there will be some students who will just not see or admit to the problem. Unfortunately, they will probably need to wait until their life is in a terrible state before they can or will do something. Remember also, that dependence on a substance can have very strong physical and psychological roots, and can be a problem that a student has had for many years. These days it is not unusual to encounter alcoholic or substance dependent students who began their use in elementary or middle school.

Eating Disorders

There are two main types of eating disorders. One involves compulsive eating and obesity. The other includes a continuum of problems that runs from chronic dieting and obsession about weight with intermittent binge eating and vomiting to severe and dangerous types of bulimia and anorexia nervosa. The two are not unrelated. The later continuum of problems is in part a reaction to the fear of obesity and the severe sanctions that our society provides, particularly to women who are even a few pounds over some ideal weight. Although obesity and compulsive eating are significant problems for some students, this discussion will focus primarily on the disorders related to losing

weight. The treatment of obesity has proven to be quite difficult and success in changing eating behavior usually requires a
structured weight-loss and behavior-change program. Students
who want to change these kinds of eating behaviors should be
referred to one of the professionally supervised weight-control
programs.

The eating disorders that are most troublesome to college
students are related to weight loss, but are usually found in
women who are not really obese. The less-severe kinds of these
eating disorders are probably developmental and relate to the
developing sense of identity that a student forms. Since thinness and beauty are so highly prized in our society it is natural
that female students would experiment with ways to achieve
this ideal. Unfortunately many of these eating disorder problems go beyond temporary experimentation and can cause great
physical and psychological harm.

Anorexia, which is typically seen in women in the mid to
late teens is a fairly obvious disorder, although it is amazing
to observe the denial that sometimes goes on in families with
an anorexic daughter. Bulimia, on the other hand, is not easy
to see. The typical bulimic student is not over- or underweight
and is often functioning very well and, in fact, is often very
active and in many leadership positions. Failure to negotiate
typical developmental needs for autonomy and separation from
parents has been associated with bulimia. Sometimes women
who are bulimic come from high-achieving, demanding families where their role as daughter and achiever was well defined.
When they get to college they begin to look for their own,
new role and are often confused and unprepared to move into
an autonomous and well-defined adult role. They use binging
and purging as a way of controlling the depression and anxiety that comes with this confusion. Since binging and purging,
at one time or another, is not uncommon among female college students, how do you determine the seriousness of this
behavior? As with most of the other personal emotional and
behavioral problems, the impact of the problem on the student
determines, in large part, how serious the disorder is at any
one time. Often bulimic behaviors, binging and purging, are
hidden and students may have been controlled by this eating
disorder for months or even years before they finally seek help

or are discovered and referred. Even though the official criteria for a diagnosis of bulimia are somewhat stringent, any form of binging and purging certainly deserves attention and probably some form of counseling. Students often move along the seriousness continuum from periodic binging and purging to regular uncontrollable behavior, so an early intervention can be helpful.

The criteria for a diagnosis of bulimia nervosa as stated in the diagnostic manual used by psychiatrists and psychologists are as follows:

A. Recurrent episodes of binge eating.
B. A feeling of lack of control over eating behaviors during the eating binges.
C. The person regularly engages in either self-induced vomiting, use of laxatives or diuretics, strict dieting or fasting, or vigorous exercise in order to prevent weight gain.
D. A minimum average of two binge-eating episodes a week for at least three months.
E. Persistent overconcern with body shape and weight.

Binging and purging is so prevalent among college women (not full-fledged bulimia) that if you are talking with a female student who is dealing with self-concept, identity, achievement, and who is hard on herself and tends to be a perfectionist, there is a strong probability that she is in some stage of an eating disorder. One of the unfortunate things about bulimic behavior is that it has become so popular that it is learned. Students actually try it as a result of reading about it or hearing about it from friends. Unfortunately for some students, learning the behavior soon leads to uncontrolled behavior and the use of binging and purging as a way to deal with stress and as a distorted way to gain personal control.

Treatment for bulimia and eating disorders in general has proven to be quite difficult. Widespread educational programs have helped stop some women from beginning this behavior and have also encouraged many to seek help. Both individual and group therapy have been effective and use of certain antidepressant drugs has also proved helpful in some cases. Counseling and therapy with persons on the serious end of the continuum is complicated and involved. It usually includes discussion of basic developmental issues and includes considerable work with early family problems and unresolved issues with parents. Treatment is further complicated when other problems like substance abuse, and histories of sexual and physical abuse are present.

The role of a faculty member or other friend or college staff member is difficult with eating-disorder students. In many cases you may either learn about the problem directly from the student or from other students who are concerned. In these cases you have something to work from and a referral with encouragement and follow-up are imperative. For most other female students with whom you will be discussing personal problems, an awareness of the prevalence of eating disorders will help you ask appropriate questions to check out the possibility of an eating disorder.

Dysfunctional Families

This discussion of dysfunctional families will include students who come from families where there was significant physical, emotional, or sexual abuse. Although most of the literature on dysfunctional families refers to people who grew up in alcoholic families, the term also fits for dysfunctions that were not caused by alcohol. In reality most physical, emotional, and sexual abuse is probably alcohol related. Students who grew up in these kinds of family situations had to learn certain ways of behaving in order to survive. Those behaviors, however, don't serve them well as adults or in healthy relationships. Students from these situations, of course, have a great variety of emotional and psychological problems, however, there are some characteristic beliefs that are often present. These include the following:

(1) **Take care of others, ignore your own needs.** Students who have grown up in families where they had to take on the role of parent because their own parents couldn't take care of them tend to want to be responsible for everyone else while ignoring their own needs. They are really reliving their childhood experience, and in a sense they don't believe that they deserve to take care of themselves.

(2) **Don't trust people, it hurts too much.** Students who grow up in a family that is untrustworthy (alcoholic, abusing

parents) learn to be wary and not to trust. As children they had too many disappointments and painful experiences when they opened themselves up to trust.

(3) **Don't allow yourself to feel anything.** If a person is beaten, sexually molested, or yelled at constantly they learn to avoid the hurt and pain by not allowing themselves to feel. Of course, as an adult this keeps a student from experiencing joy as well as pain and it creates considerable stress and internal pressure.

(4) **Don't get close to others.** A variation on the don't-trust rule, this prevents students from forming intimate relationships and from having healthy sexual relationships. Often, as a result of earlier abuse, they don't really feel that they deserve love. Unconsciously they may feel that they did something to deserve their treatment as a child.

(5) **Don't discuss personal issues or your thoughts and feelings.** In families with a terrible secret like emotional or physical abuse, everyone learns to avoid dealing with these painful issues and to pretend to the rest of the world that everything is all right.

Because of their painful past many students from dysfunctional families live a kind of pretend existence, never really believing that they are worthy or that there isn't something really wrong with them because of their past experiences. Sometimes they try to deny these past experiences so much that they aren't sure what really happened when they were children. It is not unusual for victims of child sexual abuse to believe that they dreamed that someone had sex with them or even to totally repress and deny what has happened. Sometimes they only begin to remember and face what happened when they become involved in relationships that start to generate feeling and emotion.

The recent books and media discussion of the terms dysfunctional family and ACOAs (Adult Children of Alcoholics), and the portrayal of the adult effects and ways to overcome problems have been very helpful. Students who have experienced painful childhoods because of alcoholic or other kinds of dysfunctional families have been able to learn why they feel the way they do. Learning about the symptoms and identifying them as common and not really deserved or terribly unusual, makes students feel more hopeful and often helps them gain enough hope and courage to seek help. Group counseling has proven to be very helpful to these students. A group enhances their realization that they are not alone. The encouragement and family feeling that students get in the group is also very therapeutic. Because of the rather powerful negative learning that has taken place during their childhoods, it takes considerable time for these students to overcome negative feelings and attitudes related to abuse as children. Their problems are often developmental, but they are not easily handled. In a sense their past experience has blocked prior development and they often have to go back and catch up in many life areas.

Each of the areas discussed here has generated considerable popular literature and psychological research. We will undoubtedly learn more about the frequency and variations of these experiences and also about ways to provide treatment. Although the revelations about the frequency of these problems and experiences are discouraging (at least to me), I am continually impressed with the courage and resilience that students who have experienced great pain and suffering during their childhood demonstrate. The development of support groups and a language to describe these experiences is a very hopeful sign. Since many of these kinds of problems and behaviors are passed down from generation to generation we may even be able to decrease the continuation of some of these negative family behaviors through awareness and education.

11

Professional Help and Referral

Although this chapter comes at the end of the book, the need for assessment and referral, when appropriate, has been an important theme in most of the other chapters. In general, faculty members, advisors, other staff, and friends are the first line of defense when it comes to dealing with college student problems. Most students will talk with a friend, a minister, or some other trusted advisor prior to seeking out professional help. Although more and more students and others realize that seeking counseling from a professional is an intelligent and reasonable thing to do, the stigma of seeing a "therapist" still exists for many people. This is particularly true for men. Most college counseling centers find that they have about twice as many female as male clients.

Because so many students do confide in and talk with friends and others on campus, the potential for these people to be helpful and to serve a valuable counseling role is tremendous. Although nonprofessional counselors do not have extensive training, considerable research has demonstrated their value. The usefulness of these kinds of helpers can be greatly enhanced by knowledge and training. This book was written with this fact in mind. Hopefully, the additional knowledge provided here will enhance the work of anyone who might act as a counselor to college students. I have repeatedly reinforced the value of this role and the positive possibilities, and at the same time counseled caution and attention to limits. Clearly, there are many situations when a faculty member or other person in a counseling role needs to refer students to a professional.

The assessment necessary to decide when to refer and the process of making a referral can be difficult. Assessment is particularly difficult for traditional-age students because these students often have intense and sometimes impulsive reactions to developmental problems and stressors. The person who chooses to work as a nonprofessional counselor will clearly face the dilemma, probably often, of trying to decide the seriousness of a particular problem being discussed by a student. As one of those people who takes on a counseling role you will also face the problem of being involved with, and committed to the student, no matter what the problem. I mention these realities again because I believe that it is crucial for the nonprofessional counselor to choose his or her involvements judiciously. Some faculty members and others on campus, realizing the difficulties of personal involvement, choose not to get involved with students at all. Given the realities of tenure, and other personal and job responsibilities, this decision may be justified, although my ideal is a campus where everyone takes some responsibility for helping students.

In earlier discussions of the assessment and referral process I may not have emphasized the importance of having a professional consultant as strongly as is necessary. If you as a friend, advisor, faculty member, or other person in the college community decide to take on a counseling role for students, you need to have easy access to professional backup. You must have someone whom you can trust available to consult with about difficult situations with students. This person will most likely be a campus counselor, psychologist, or psychiatrist. On most campuses these people are very willing to help and to advise you; however, they are often in short supply and contacting them sometimes takes persistence. I would recommend the strategy of picking out one person to use as a regular consultant. This will not always be possible since you may be faced with an urgent situation in which you need to get to anyone available. If you don't have anyone readily available to you, then working in a counseling capacity as a nonprofessional is a very tricky business.

Another important prerequisite is training. Although I have attempted to provide information on the counseling process, college student development, and the college environment; hands-on training is also highly recommended. A training course in counseling skills where you can work with a professional instructor and other trainees to get feedback on your own verbal and nonverbal responses can be extremely valuable. This training is not routinely offered by colleges and universities for faculty and other staff, although some counseling and mental health centers do offer relevant workshops.

Before discussing the referral process itself in some detail, it is important to provide some description of the different mental health facilities typically available on campus. I have mentioned counseling and mental health centers as common to most campuses. Generally speaking, a college or university will provide some level of personal and career counseling for students. Usually these facilities are part of the general student affairs program or are located within the campus health facility. The support and funding vary considerably and most of these centers offer limited services and short-term counseling. It is important to realize that a referral to one of these counselors may well result in yet another referral. Usually, if the student needs extensive psychotherapy he or she will have to be referred to a private mental health practitioner. Sometimes it may make sense to consult with the campus counseling and mental health personnel to ascertain if a referral directly to an outside therapist should be made.

Attempting to make a referral to a mental health therapist in the community can be confusing. There are many different categories of mental health workers and these therapists often have particular expertise in specific areas. My approach is generally to pay more attention to the therapist's expertise and personal ability than to a particular degree category, although there are times when a referral might be appropriate only for certain types of therapists. Following is a brief review of the major categories of therapists that you might consider, their background, and some information about their general areas of expertise:

Counseling and Clinical Psychologists. They usually need a Ph.D. to be licensed. This requires extensive academic work in psychology, psychological testing, and the counseling/therapy process. They are required to have a one-year internship in most states and a year of supervised practice after the completion of their degree. Psychologists are usually trained to deal with a wide range of human problems and psychopathology. Not able to prescribe drugs.

Psychiatrists. They are medical doctors who specialize in emotional and psychological problems. Most practicing psychiatrists have completed at least a three-year residency training in psychiatry and are trained to deal with a wide range of emotional and psychological problems. They have experience and training with severely disturbed patients, usually in both in- and outpatient settings. Their medical training gives them particular expertise in understanding the physical components of psychiatric problems. Many use drugs to relieve symptoms and to treat emotional and behavioral problems.

Ministers, Chaplains, and Pastoral Counselors. They usually have a theological degree with varying amounts of formal training in psychology and counseling. Pastoral Counselors usually have at least the equivalent of a master's level training in counseling and psychotherapy. These counselors often have experience in working with families and, of course, can be particularly helpful in discussing spiritual problems and issues. I do not recommend "fundamentalist" religious counselors who tend to provide answers in accordance with an inflexible religious doctrine, although sometimes students from fundamentalist backgrounds respond well to being given the "answers" to life problems.

Mental Health Counselors, Psychiatric Social Workers, Marriage and Family Counselors. This category encompasses a large number of counselors. Most often these counselors have a master's degree and some level of formal supervised training. Sometimes their training is somewhat specialized, as in the case of marriage and family counselors. These therapists are now licensed in many states where requirements for training are enforced. Generally they do not have training that is as extensive as psychiatrists and psychologists, although some of them may have doctoral degrees that require training of a similar length.

As I mentioned before, the title itself is not that helpful as a guideline for referral. Your best bet, if you have access to a knowledgeable consultant, is to find out about the expertise and particular skills of local therapists before referring. Because counseling and psychotherapy is such a personal process, having the necessary credentials doesn't necessarily mean that a therapist will be able to work with a particular student.

The referral process itself includes a number of stages. Each of these will be described in some detail in the following section. The stages include: (1) rapport building, (2) assessment, (3) deciding to refer, (4) determining an appropriate referral, (5) making the referral and dealing with resistance, and (6) follow-up.

(1) Rapport Building

Even if a referral seems like an obvious decision within the first minute or two of a discussion with a troubled student, the rapport between you as the person making the referral and the student is crucial. Students are frequently hypersensitive to being "shuffled" to someone else. Too often our bureaucratic campus organizations make it difficult for a student to get information or help. The experience of being in this kind of a system, plus the inherent difficulties involved in telling anyone else about a personal problem or difficulty, and the stigma that still exists for many students regarding professional counselors or therapists, makes referral very difficult. The relationship between the student being referred and the referring person can mean the difference between an effective and an ineffective referral. Many students who are referred to a counselor never get there. They may become angry at the person suggesting the referral, or they may just be too scared to take yet another step.

Once again, there is a rather delicate balance for the advisor, faculty member, or person working in a counseling capacity. On the one hand, it doesn't make sense to spend time getting involved with a student who must be referred to a professional counselor or psychologist, and on the other hand a student who, for any number of reasons, is hesitant to seek professional help is not likely to take advice unless he or she trusts the advice giver. The best course of action here, I believe, is for the person making the referral to be sure to spend time establishing a rapport and building trust. Perhaps a good rule of thumb is never to make a referral during the first few minutes of a conversation with a student, or, if one is made early, to continue to discuss the student's feelings and situation for a while.

(2) Assessment

Often it will be obvious just from the initial statement of a problem that a student needs professional help. Assessment in those cases is not difficult. In many kinds of situations, many of which have been discussed in previous chapters, an assessment of the student's situation is important prior to a decision to refer. This assessment will probably include some focus on the *seriousness* of the student's problem as well as on the *complexity* and *chronicity* of the situation. In most cases a person who is a nonprofessional counselor will not want to deal with problems that are too serious, too involved, or too chronic. As I have discussed in previous chapters, situational and developmental problems are most appropriate for nonprofessional counselors. If a student is undergoing a difficult period and needs support or help clarifying ways to cope, then a faculty member or other person working as a counselor can probably be most effective. If a student has more serious problems such as physical symptoms related to stress, acute depression, or long-standing self-worth difficulties, professional help is needed.

It should be obvious from the discussion of assessment in previous chapters that there are no absolute rules. When in doubt it is best to consult with a professional and perhaps, if the student is amenable, arrange a one-session "talk" with the professional for evaluation. It may be that after the evaluation, the professional counselor will encourage further contact between you and the student.

(3) Deciding to Refer

The decision to refer should be based upon an assessment of the student's situation *and* upon the circumstances of the person serving as counselor. Personal feelings and time constraints of the faculty member, minister, or other person working with students must enter into the decision. As I emphasized earlier, the decision or commitment to counsel a student should be conscious and deliberate. The same is true of a referral. If a decision is made that a referral is necessary (for whatever reasons), then it's important to stick to it even if the student refuses the referral or resists it.

(4) Determining an Appropriate Referral

Hopefully resources are available for referral on or near your campus. Prior to making a referral you should have a good idea of who and what is available, as well as some understanding of what the student will have to go through in order to see someone. Will there be forms to fill out? A long wait? Will the counselor be familiar with this particular kind of problem? If you, as the referring person, are unsure of any aspects of the process, you need to become informed prior to talking with the student. Again, consulting with a professional can be helpful. A familiarization visit to the mental health or counseling agency will help you get a feel for what will actually happen to the student.

If the referral will be off campus you may want to discuss the case with the potential therapist prior to referring the student. This is a perfectly acceptable practice, although it may be difficult to reach a private therapist by phone. There is an ethical issue to consider regarding your consulting about the student without his or her permission. Professional therapists are bound by ethics to obtain the client's permission prior to discussing their case, but this restriction does not apply to nonprofessionals working in a counseling capacity. I would recommend, however, that in cases where it is not possible or practical to get the student's permission, his or her identity be kept confidential when the case is discussed with possible therapists.

(5) Making the Referral and Dealing with Resistance

This is certainly the touchiest part of the process. In essence, by suggesting to the student that he or she needs to see a professional therapist, you are telling him or her that his or her problem is serious and needs professional attention. There is no real way to avoid this rather direct communication of your concern. People often find it difficult. It requires the person doing the referral to be honest about a difficult judgment call. As a person referring, you might be wrong. You might be over-reacting, but if this is so at least you will have erred in a positive direction. The student may be angry or embarrassed, but he or she will also respect your concern and courage. I believe that a direct approach is better than an indirect one, where you hide the real reason for the referral and perhaps cloak it in some other terms. This is not to say that you need to be painfully frank or that you need share your most negative assessment with the student. For example, if a student is depressed and has some serious symptoms of depression, the referring counselor might say something like, "Jack, you have been depressed for several weeks and I really think that you need to go over to the counseling center and get some professional advice." It is very helpful to be able to refer to a specific person. Typically you would know this person and be able to communicate a positive feeling about the counselor to the student. In some counseling centers and clinic situations this may not be possible because of their operating systems. It is also helpful to prepare the student for his or her first visit. This can be done by discussing the counseling process and helping the student learn about what to expect from the first visit. Many students don't really under-stand much about counseling, and they may have the image of a "Freud-like" figure who will put them on a couch and ask questions about their mothers. Or worse yet, their images of counseling, psychologists, or psychiatrists come from television, where most therapists are portrayed as buffoons.

Your personal attitudes about counseling and therapy will be communicated to the student in one way or another. If you have little confidence or feel anxious and negative about what will happen to the student, this will come across. If you do have a healthy degree of skepticism, it is probably better to own up to it than to be insincere. Usually, the students themselves will be skeptical and one of the professional counselor's first tasks is to allay the client's fears and demonstrate understanding and expertise.

In some cases, when you know that the student is in great need and he or she seems likely to follow instructions, the best approach may be a rather authoritative one. For these students you can pick up the phone, make an appointment for the student, and instruct them to be there at the appointed time, leaving no room for argument or resistance. This approach can, of course, backfire if the student reacts negatively to your directness.

What do you do when a student refuses a referral and leaves your office? What if you believe that the student is in really bad shape and shouldn't be left to fend for him- or herself? In this case the best approach is probably to discuss the situation with the dean of students or the administrative officer responsible for student services. He or she may decide to call the student in, to involve parents, or even to require counseling. If possible you should inform the student that you are concerned enough about his or her welfare that you are taking this step.

In nonemergency cases when a student refuses to accept a referral, you will be faced with the decision of what to do next. Since you have made the decision that the student needs to be referred, it is no longer appropriate for you to continue counseling the student. It may be tough for the student to accept this and it may be difficult for you to "cut off" the student. In the long run you and the student will be better off if you stick to your referral decision. The student may not be ready to confront his or her problem and your firmness in emphasizing the importance of the referral may be significant. Also, your own mental health will be enhanced if you are not forced to deal with a student who needs professional help.

(6) Follow-up

A large percentage of referrals are never acted upon. Students will often agree that they need help, but will never really take the next step and go to a counseling or mental health center. In one sense, the decision is theirs, and the person making the referral suggestion must leave it to their judgment. On the other hand, particularly if the student is in serious trouble, the faculty member or other person making the referral has some ongoing obligation to follow up and make every effort possible to get help for the student. I would suggest two different courses of action, one for noncritical situations and one for those times when a student's situation is critical and he or she must get help soon.

For noncritical cases, the person making the referral should follow up in a week or two by asking the student if he or she has gotten in to see someone. If he or she hasn't, then a bit more push is probably in order. You can ask if it is difficult or if he or she would like you to call and make the appointment. Actually, even for noncritical situations it is not a bad idea to call and make the appointment for the student. This may be a bit too pushy, but it increases the likelihood that the student will at least show up for an initial appointment. At some point the student will still have to decide if he or she really wants to go ahead with counseling, but taking that first step is a big barrier for many students.

In emergency and critical situations, you basically have to take on responsibility for seeing that the student gets counseling or for informing a dean or someone in the student-services administration of the situation. Often, a student who is seriously disturbed does not have the judgment necessary to make a decision about getting help, and he or she needs to be forced into some kind of treatment. In the long run this may not work, but at least every opportunity for assistance is being made for the student.

This book has included a great deal of information and probably too much advice. I have tried not to use too much jargon and at the same time not to oversimplify. In a way, any attempt to describe and discuss human behavior is an oversimplification. I have tried to give examples and to provide generalizations that will be useful. Of course, generalizations don't always work for individual students. Although I have repeatedly suggested professional counseling as an option, I realize that most students get along on their own or with a little help from their friends. Obviously, I am biased toward the value of counseling and one of my main purposes in writing this book was to try to encourage and assist many different people on college campuses to take on a counseling role. Students, particularly traditional-age ones, are undergoing very significant developmental experiences, and a little help at the right time can make a profound difference in their lives.

I have tried to make what I have written applicable to both traditional-age and adult students, although much of what I have offered seems to be related more directly to younger students. I probably haven't stressed the importance of gender, ethnic, and racial differences as much as I should. Certainly, these factors have very significant influences on a student's experiences, and anyone attempting to counsel students must work as hard as he or she can to understand and respond to cultural background and socialization. In addition to learning about general counseling techniques, it can be very useful for potential counselors to seek training in understanding gender, cultural, and racial differences. Many problems on contemporary college campuses are emerging in these areas, and workshops and special training and awareness sessions are often available.

I have written this book in a somewhat informal style and I feel compelled to somehow say good-bye to the reader. I hope that you have found what you have read useful. If you are someone who is willing to take the extra time to work with individual students and talk with them about their lives, their hopes, and their problems, I congratulate you for your compassion and caring.

THE CONTINUUM
COUNSELING LIBRARY
Books of Related Interest

_____Denyse Beaudet
ENCOUNTERING THE MONSTER
Pathways in Children's Dreams
Based on original empirical research, and with recourse to the
works of Jung, Neumann, Eliade, Marie-Louise Franz, and
others, this book offers proven methods of approaching and
understanding the dream life of children. $17.95

_____Robert W. Buckingham
CARE OF THE DYING CHILD
A Practical Guide for Those Who Help Others
"Buckingham's book delivers a powerful, poignant message
deserving a wide readership."—*Library Journal* $17.95

_____Alastair V. Campbell, ed.
A DICTIONARY OF PASTORAL CARE
Provides information on the essentials of counseling and the
kinds of problems encountered in pastoral practice. The approach is interdenominational and interdisciplinary. Contains
over 300 entries by 185 authors in the fields of theology, philoso-
phy, psychology, and sociology as well as from the theoretical
background of psychotherapy and counseling. $24.50

_____David A. Crenshaw
BEREAVEMENT
Counseling the Grieving throughout the Life Cycle
Grief is examined from a life cycle perspective, infancy to old
age. Special losses and practical strategies for frontline
caregivers highlight this comprehensive guidebook. $17.95

_____Reuben Fine
THE HISTORY OF PSYCHOANALYSIS
New Expanded Edition
"Objective, comprehensive, and readable. A rare work. Highly
recommended, whether as an introduction to the field or as a
fresh overview to those already familiar with it."—*Contemporary
Psychology* $24.95 paperback

_____Reuben Fine
LOVE AND WORK
The Value System of Psychoanalysis
One of the world's leading authorities on Freud sheds new light
on psychoanalysis as a process for releasing the power of love.
$24.95

_____Raymond B. Flannery, Jr.
BECOMING STRESS-RESISTANT
Through the Project SMART Program
"An eminently practical book with the goals of helping men and
women of the 1990s make changes in their lives."—Charles V.
Ford, Academy of Psychosomatic Medicine $17.95

_____Lucy Freeman
FIGHT AGAINST FEARS
With a new Introduction by
Flora Rheta Schreiber
More than a million copies sold. The new—and only available—
edition of the first, and still best, true story of a modern woman's
journey of self-discovery through psychoanalysis.
$10.95 paperback

_____Lucy Freeman
OUR INNER WORLD OF RAGE
Understanding and Transforming the Power of Anger
A psychoanalytic examination of the anger that burns within us
and which can be used to save or slowly destroy us. Sheds light
on all expressions of rage, from the murderer to the suicide to
those of us who feel depressed and angry but are unaware of the
real cause. $9.95 paperback

_____ John Gerdtz and Joel Bregman, M. D.
AUTISM
A Practical Guide for Those Who Help Others
An up-to-date and comprehensive guidebook for everyone who
works with autistic children, adolescents, adults, and their
families. Includes latest information on medications. $17.95

_____Marion Howard
HOW TO HELP YOUR TEENAGER
POSTPONE SEXUAL INVOLVEMENT
Based on a national educational program that works, this book
advises parents, teachers, and counselors on how they can help
their teens resist social and peer pressures regarding sex.
$9.95 paperback

_____Marion Howard
SOMETIMES I WONDER ABOUT ME
Teenagers and Mental Health
Combines fictional narratives with sound, understandable
professional advice to help teenagers recognize the difference
between serious problems and normal problems of adjustment.
$9.95 paperback

_____Charles H. Huber and Barbara A. Backlund
THE TWENTY MINUTE COUNSELOR
Transforming Brief Conversations into Effective
Helping Experiences
Expert advice for anyone who by necessity must often counsel
"on the run" or in a short period of time. $16.95

_____E. Clay Jorgensen
CHILD ABUSE
A Practical Guide for Those Who Help Others
Essential information and practical advice for caregivers called
upon to help both child and parent in child abuse. $16.95

_____Eugene Kennedy
CRISIS COUNSELING
The Essential Guide for Nonprofessional Counselors
"An outstanding author of books on personal growth selects
types of personal crises that our present life-style has made
commonplace and suggests effective ways to deal with them."
—*Best Sellers* $10.95

_____Eugene Kennedy and Sara Charles, M. D.
ON BECOMING A COUNSELOR
A Basic Guide for Nonprofessional Counselors
New expanded edition of an indispensable resource. A patient-
oriented, clinically directed field guide to understanding and
responding to troubled people. $27.95 hardcover
$15.95 paperback

_____Eugene Kennedy
SEXUAL COUNSELING
A Practical Guide for Those Who Help Others
Newly revised and up-to-date edition, with a new chapter on
the counselor and AIDS, of an essential book on counseling
people with sexual problems. $17.95

_____Bonnie Lester
WOMEN AND AIDS
A Practical Guide for Those Who Help Others
Provides positive ways for women to deal with their fears, and
to help others who react with fear to people who have AIDS.
$15.95

_____Robert J. Lovinger
RELIGION AND COUNSELING
The Psychological Impact of Religious Belief
How counselors and clergy can best understand the important
emotional significance of religious thoughts and feelings. $17.95

_____ Sophie Lovinger, Mary Ellen Brandell, and
Linda Seestedt-Stanford
LANGUAGE LEARNING DISABILITIES
*A New and Practical Approach for Those Who Work with
Children and Their Families*
Here is new information, together with practical suggestions, on
how teachers, therapists, and families can work together to give
learning disabled children new strengths. $17.95

_____Helen B. McDonald and Audrey I. Steinhorn
HOMOSEXUALITY
A Practical Guide to Counseling Lesbians, Gay Men, and Their Families
A sensitive guide to better understanding and counseling gays, lesbians, and their parents, at every stage of their lives. $17.95

_____ James McGuirk and Mary Elizabeth McGuirk
FOR WANT OF A CHILD
A Psychologist and His Wife Explore the Emotional Effects and Challenges of Infertility
A new understanding of infertility that comes from one couple's lived experience, as well as sound professional advice for couples and counselors. $17.95

_____ Janice N. McLean and Sheila A. Knights
PHOBICS AND OTHER PANIC VICTIMS
A Practical Guide for Those Who Help Them
"A must for the phobic, spouse and family, and for the physician and support people who help them." — Arthur B. Hardy, M. D., Founder, TERRAP Phobia Program $17.95

_____ John B. Mordock and William Van Ornum
CRISIS COUNSELING WITH CHILDREN AND ADOLESCENTS
A Guide for Nonprofessional Counselors
New Expanded Edition
"Every parent should keep this book on the shelf right next to the nutrition, medical, and Dr. Spock books."—*Marriage & Family Living* $12.95

_____ John B. Mordock
COUNSELING CHILDREN
Basic Principles for Helping the Troubled and Defiant Child
Helps counselors consider the best route for a particular child, and offers proven principles and methods to counsel troubled children in a variety of situations. $17.95

_____Cherry Boone O'Neill
DEAR CHERRY
Questions and Answers on Eating Disorders
Practical and inspiring advice on eating disorders from the best-
selling author of *Starving for Attention.* $8.95 paperback

_____Paul G. Quinnett
ON BECOMING A HEALTH
AND HUMAN SERVICES MANAGER
A Practical Guide for Clinicians and Counselors
A new and essential guide to management for everyone in the
helping professions—from mental health to nursing, from social
work to teaching. $19.95

_____Paul G. Quinnett
SUICIDE: THE FOREVER DECISION
For Those Thinking About Suicide,
and For Those Who Know, Love, or Counsel Them
"A treasure— this book can help save lives."—William Van
Ornum, psychotherapist and author $18.95 hardcover
$8.95 paperback

_____Paul G. Quinnett
WHEN SELF-HELP FAILS
A Consumer's Guide to Counseling Services
A guide to professional therapie. "Without a doubt one of the
most honest, reassuring, nonpaternalistic, and useful self-help
books ever to appear."—*Booklist* $10.95

_____ Judah L. Ronch
ALZHEIMER'S DISEASE
A Practical Guide for Families and Other Caregivers
Must reading for everyone who must deal with the effects of this
tragic disease on a daily basis. Filled with examples as well as
facts, this book provides insights into dealing with one's feelings
as well as with such practical advice as how to choose long-term
care. $11.95 paperback

_____Theodore Isaac Rubin, M. D.
ANTI-SEMITISM : A DISEASE OF THE MIND
"A most poignant and lucid psychological examination of a
severe emotional disease. Dr. Rubin offers hope and under-
standing to the victim and to the bigot. A splendid job!"
—Dr. Herbert S. Strean $14.95

_____Theodore Isaac Rubin, M.D.
CHILD POTENTIAL
Fulfilling Your Child's Intellectual, Emotional, and Creative Promise
Information, guidance, and wisdom—a treasury of fresh ideas
for parents to help their children become their best selves
without professional help. $18.95

_____ John R. Shack
COUPLES COUNSELING
A Practical Guide for Those Who Help Others
An essential guide to dealing with the 20 percent of all counsel-
ing situations that involve the relationship of two people. $17.95

_____ Herbert S. Strean as told to Lucy Freeman
BEHIND THE COUCH
Revelations of a Psychoanalyst
A leading psychoanalyst reveals what it feels like to be behind
the couch. $11.95 paperback

_____Stuart Sutherland
THE INTERNATIONAL DICTIONARY OF PSYCHOLOGY
This new dictionary of psychology also covers a wide range of
related disciplines, from anthropology to sociology. $49.95

_____ Joan Leslie Taylor
IN THE LIGHT OF DYING
The Journals of a Hospice Volunteer
"Beautifully recounts the healing (our own) that results from
service to others, and might well be considered as required
reading for hospice volunteers." —Stephen Levine, author of
Who Dies? $17.95

_____Montague Ullman, M. D. and Claire Limmer, M. S., eds.
THE VARIETY OF DREAM EXPERIENCE
Expanding Our Ways of Working With Dreams
"Lucidly describes the beneficial impact dream analysis can have
in diverse fields and in society as a whole."—*Booklist*
$19.95 hardcover $14.95 paperback

_____William Van Ornum and Mary W. Van Ornum
TALKING TO CHILDREN ABOUT NUCLEAR WAR
"A wise book. A needed book. An urgent book."
—Dr. Karl A. Menninger $15.95 hardcover $7.95 paperback

_____Kathleen Zraly and David Swift, M. D.
ANOREXIA, BULIMIA, AND COMPULSIVE OVEREATING
A Practical Guide for Counselors and Families
New and helpful approaches for everyone who knows, loves, or
counsels victims of anorexia, bulimia, and chronic overeating.
$17.95

At your bookstore, or to order directly, send your check or
money order (adding $2.00 extra per book for postage and
handling, up to $6.00 maximum) to: The Continuum Publishing
Company, 370 Lexington Avenue, New York, NY , 10017. Prices
are subject to change.